Home
BAKER

More than 160
baking recipes

DK

DK | Penguin Random House

Project Editor Elizabeth Yeates
Designers Alison Shackleton, Saskia Janssen
Senior Jacket Creative Mark Penfound
Pre-Production Producer Rebecca Fallowfield
Producer Konrad Kirkham
Special Sales Creative Project Manager
Alison Donovan

First published in Great Britain in 2015 by
Dorling Kindersley Limited,
80 Strand, London WC2R 0RL

Material previously published in
Cooking Through the Year (2012),
Family Kitchen Cookbook (2013), Biscuits &
Traybakes (2014), and Pizzas & Flatbreads (2014)

A CIP catalogue record for this book
is available from the British Library.
ISBN 978-0-2412-0118-3

Printed in China

All images © Dorling Kindersley Limited
For further information see: www.dkimages.com

A WORLD OF IDEAS:
SEE ALL THERE IS TO KNOW

Contents

Cakes and muffins

Victoria sponge cake

Probably the most iconic British cake, a good Victoria sponge should be well-risen, moist, and as light as air.

🥣 **30 MINS**

🍲 **20-25 MINS**

❄️ **FREEZABLE**

SPECIAL EQUIPMENT

2 x 18cm (7in) round cake tins

SERVES 6-8

175g (6oz) unsalted butter, softened, plus extra for greasing

175g (6oz) caster sugar

3 eggs

1 tsp vanilla extract

175g (6oz) self-raising flour

1 tsp baking powder

FOR THE FILLING

50g (1¾oz) unsalted butter, softened

100g (3½oz) icing sugar, plus extra for dusting

1 tsp vanilla extract

115g (4oz) good-quality seedless raspberry jam

1 Preheat the oven to 180°C (350°F/Gas 4). Grease two 18cm (7in) round cake tins and line with baking parchment. Whisk the butter and sugar in a bowl for 2 minutes, or until pale, light, and fluffy. Add the eggs 1 at a time, mixing well between additions to avoid curdling.

2 Add the vanilla extract, and whisk briefly until it is well-blended through the batter. Whisk the mixture for another 2 minutes until bubbles appear on the surface. Remove the whisk, then sift the flour and baking powder into the bowl.

3 With a metal spoon, gently fold in the flour until just smooth; try to keep the mixture light. Divide the mixture evenly between the tins and smooth the tops with a palette knife. Cook for 20–25 minutes, or until golden brown and springy to the touch.

4 Test the sponges by inserting a metal skewer into the centre of both cakes. If it comes out clean, the cakes are cooked. Remove

from the oven and leave them for a few minutes in the tins. Turn out, good sides up, onto a wire rack to cool completely.

5 For the filling, beat together the butter, icing sugar, and vanilla extract until smooth. Continue to beat for up to 5 minutes until the buttercream is very light, cloud-like, and fluffy in texture.

6 Spread the buttercream evenly onto the flat side of a cooled sponge with a palette knife. Gently spread the jam on top of the buttercream using a table knife. Top with the second sponge, so that the flat sides are together. Serve as soon as possible, dusted with sifted icing sugar.

Layered carrot cake

This rich, heavily iced cake is multi-layered, and makes a really impressive centrepiece at a special tea party.

⏱ 30 MINS

🍲 40 MINS

❄ FREEZABLE

SPECIAL EQUIPMENT

2 x 22cm (8½ in) springform cake tins

electric hand-held whisk

SERVES 10

150g (5½ oz) walnuts

450ml (15fl oz) sunflower oil, plus extra for greasing

6 large eggs, lightly beaten

2 tsp vanilla extract

450g (1lb) soft light brown sugar

350g (12oz) finely grated carrots

150g (5½ oz) sultanas

550g (1¼ lb) self-raising flour, sifted

½ tsp salt

2 tsp ground cinnamon

2 tsp ground ginger

finely grated zest of 1 large orange

FOR THE ICING

150g (5½ oz) butter, softened

150g (5½ oz) cream cheese

600g (1lb 5oz) icing sugar, sifted

finely grated zest of 2 oranges

2 tsp vanilla extract

1 Preheat the oven to 180°C (350°F/Gas 4). Grease two 22cm (8½ in) springform cake tins and line the bases with baking parchment. Spread the walnuts on a baking tray and toast in the oven for about 5 minutes, until lightly browned, watching carefully that they don't burn. Put the nuts into a clean tea towel, rub them to get rid of excess skin, then set aside to cool.

2 In a large bowl, whisk together the oil, eggs, vanilla extract, and sugar with an electric hand-held whisk until light, fluffy, and thickened. Put the grated carrot in a clean tea towel and squeeze out any excess liquid, then fold it into the cake batter until evenly mixed through.

3 Roughly chop the cooled walnuts and fold them into the mixture with the sultanas. Finally fold in the flour, salt, spices, and orange zest and mix to combine.

4 Divide the mixture between the tins, and bake in the centre of the oven for 45 minutes, or until springy to the touch and a skewer inserted into the middle comes out clean from both cakes.

5 Leave the cakes to cool for 5 minutes in their tins, then turn them out to cool completely on a wire rack. Once they are cool, halve each cake horizontally using a serrated knife to give you 4 layers of cake in total, being careful to keep the layers an even thickness.

6 To make the icing, cream together the butter, cream cheese, icing sugar, orange zest, and vanilla extract. Sandwich each layer of the cake together with a scant one-fifth of the icing and cover the top and sides of the cake with the remaining icing.

Coffee and walnut cake

This is the perfect accompaniment to morning coffee. Here the cake is made in small tins to give it extra height.

🥣 20 MINS

🍲 20-25 MINS

❄ FREEZABLE

SPECIAL EQUIPMENT

2 x 17cm (6¾ in) round cake tins

electric hand-held whisk

SERVES 8

175g (6oz) unsalted butter, softened, plus extra for greasing

175g (6oz) soft light brown sugar

3 eggs

1 tsp vanilla extract

175g (6oz) self-raising flour

1 tsp baking powder

1 tbsp coffee powder, mixed with 2 tbsp boiling water and cooled

FOR THE ICING

100g (3½ oz) unsalted butter, softened

200g (7oz) icing sugar

9 walnut halves

1 Preheat the oven to 180°C (350°F/Gas 4). Grease two 17cm (6¾ in) round cake tins and line the bases with baking parchment. Cream together the butter and sugar in a bowl, using an electric hand-held whisk, until the mixture is light and fluffy.

2 Add the eggs one at a time, beating well between additions. Add the vanilla, and whisk for 2 minutes until bubbles appear on the surface. Sift in the flour and baking powder.

3 Gently fold in the flour, followed by half the coffee mixture. Divide the batter evenly between the prepared tins and smooth the tops with a palette knife.

4 Cook for 20–25 minutes, or until golden brown and springy to the touch. Test by inserting a skewer: if it comes out clean, the cakes are cooked. Leave for a few minutes, then turn out onto a wire rack to cool completely.

5 To make the icing, beat the butter and icing sugar together for 5 minutes until smooth and fluffy. Beat in the remaining coffee. Spread half the buttercream evenly over the flat side of the least good-looking of the cakes.

6 Top with the second cake, flat sides together, and spread with the remaining buttercream. Decorate with the walnut halves.

Genoise sponge with raspberries and cream

This delicate sponge makes an impressive dessert, and is also perfect as the centrepiece for an afternoon tea.

🥄 **30 MINS**

🍲 **25-30 MINS**

❄ **FREEZABLE**

SPECIAL EQUIPMENT

20cm (8in) round springform cake tin

electric hand-held whisk

SERVES 8-10

145g (1½ oz) unsalted butter, melted and cooled, plus extra for greasing

4 large eggs, lightly beaten

125g (4½ oz) caster sugar

125g (4½ oz) plain flour

1 tsp vanilla extract

finely grated zest of 1 lemon

FOR THE FILLING

450ml (15fl oz) double or whipping cream

325g (11oz) raspberries, plus 75g (2½ oz) extra, to decorate (optional)

1 tbsp icing sugar, plus extra for dusting

1 Preheat the oven to 180°C (350°F/Gas 4). Lightly grease a 20cm (8in) round springform cake tin and line the base only with baking parchment.

2 Bring a pan of water to the boil, remove from the heat, and stand a heatproof bowl over the top. Add the eggs and sugar and whisk, using an electric hand-held whisk, for 5 minutes, until the whisk leaves a trail when lifted; the mixture will expand up to 5 times its original volume. Remove the bowl from the pan and whisk for another minute to cool.

3 Sift in the flour and carefully fold it into the mixture. Fold in the vanilla, lemon zest, and melted butter.

4 Pour the batter into the prepared tin and bake for 25–30 minutes, or until the top is springy and light golden brown. A skewer should come out clean.

5 Leave the cake to cool in its tin for a few minutes, then turn out onto a wire rack and cool completely. Remove the parchment.

6 When the cake is cold, carefully cut it horizontally into 3 equal pieces, using a serrated bread knife.

7 For the filling, in a large bowl, whip the cream until stiff. Lightly crush the raspberries with the icing sugar and fold into the cream roughly, leaving behind any juice so the cream is not too wet; some pieces should look rippled.

8 Place the bottom slice of cake on a serving plate and spread with half the cream mixture. Top with the second slice, press down gently, spread with the remaining cream, and then place the final slice on top. Decorate with the raspberries (if using) and dust the cake with icing sugar. Serve the cake immediately.

Rhubarb and ginger upside-down cake

Young rhubarb is cooked into a simple upside-down cake to give a modern twist on a classic dessert.

40 MINS

40-45 MINS

SPECIAL EQUIPMENT

23cm (9in) round springform
cake tin

electric hand whisk or mixer

SERVES 6-8

150g (5½ oz) unsalted butter,
softened

150g (5½ oz) dark soft brown sugar

4 tbsp finely chopped, preserved
stem ginger

500g (1lb 2oz) young, pink rhubarb,
chopped into 2cm (¾ in) lengths

3 large eggs

150g (5½ oz) self-raising flour

2 tsp ground ginger

1 tsp baking powder

double cream, whipped, or crème
fraîche, to serve (optional)

1 Preheat the oven to 180°C
(350°F/Gas 4). Melt a little
butter and use to grease the
tin with a brush. Line the base
and sides of the cake tin with
baking parchment.

2 Scatter a little of the sugar
evenly over the base of the
cake tin. Scatter half of the
chopped stem ginger evenly over
the sugar. Lay the rhubarb over the
sugar and ginger so it is tightly
packed and completely covers
the base of the cake tin.

3 Place the butter and remaining
sugar in a large mixing bowl
and whisk with an electric hand
whisk or mixer until pale and
creamy. Beat in the eggs, one at a
time, whisking as much air as
possible into the mixture. Gently
fold the remaining chopped stem
ginger into the batter.

4 In a separate bowl, sift
together the flour, ground
ginger, and baking powder. Add
the sifted ingredients to the bowl
containing the cake batter. Gently
fold in the dry ingredients, keeping
volume in the batter as you do so.
Spoon the cake batter into the
cake tin, taking care not to disturb
the arranged rhubarb, and spread it
evenly with a palette knife.

5 Bake the cake in the centre of
the oven for 45 minutes until
springy to the touch. Remove from
the oven and leave to cool for
20–30 minutes before carefully
turning the cake out of the tin and
onto a serving plate. Serve warm
with whipped double cream or
crème fraîche.

Ginger cake

Deeply flavoured with preserved ginger, this rich and moist cake is a firm favourite.

20 MINS

20-35 MINS

FREEZABLE

SPECIAL EQUIPMENT

18cm (7in) square cake tin

SERVES 12

100g (3½ oz) unsalted butter,
softened, plus extra for greasing

225g (8oz) golden syrup

110g (4oz) soft dark brown sugar

200ml (7fl oz) whole milk

4 tbsp syrup from preserved
ginger jar

finely grated zest of 1 orange

225g (8oz) self-raising flour

1 tsp bicarbonate of soda

1 tsp mixed spice

1 tsp ground cinnamon

2 tsp ground ginger

4 pieces of preserved stem ginger,
finely chopped, and tossed in
1 tbsp plain flour

1 egg, lightly beaten

1 Preheat the oven to 170°C
(340°F/Gas 3½). Grease an
18cm (7in) square cake tin and line
the base with baking parchment.

2 In a saucepan, gently heat
the butter, golden syrup,
sugar, milk, and ginger syrup
until the butter has melted.
Add the orange zest and leave
to cool for 5 minutes.

3 In a large mixing bowl, sift
together the flour, bicarbonate
of soda, and ground spices. Pour
the warm syrup mixture into the
dry ingredients and beat them
well, using a balloon whisk. Stir
in the preserved ginger and egg.

4 Pour the batter into the tin and
cook for 35–45 minutes, until a
skewer inserted into the middle of
the cake comes out clean. Leave to
cool in the tin for at least 1 hour
before turning out onto a wire rack.
Remove the baking parchment
before serving.

German apple cake

This simple apple cake is transformed into something special with a warmly spiced, crumbly streusel topping.

30 MINS PLUS CHILLING

45-50 MINS

SPECIAL EQUIPMENT

20cm (8in) loose-bottomed cake tin

SERVES 6-8

175g (6oz) unsalted butter, softened, plus extra for greasing

175g (6oz) light muscovado sugar

finely grated zest of 1 lemon

3 eggs, lightly beaten

175g (6oz) self-raising flour

3 tbsp milk

2 tart dessert apples, peeled, cored, and cut into even, slim wedges

FOR THE STREUSEL TOPPING

115g (4oz) plain flour

85g (3oz) light muscovado sugar

2 tsp ground cinnamon

85g (3oz) unsalted butter, in pieces

1 To make the topping, put the flour, sugar, and cinnamon in a mixing bowl. Rub in the butter gently with your fingertips to form a crumbly ball of dough. Wrap the streusel dough in cling film and chill in the fridge for 30 minutes.

2 Preheat the oven to 190°C (375°F/Gas 5). Grease a 20cm (8in) loose-bottomed cake tin and line with baking parchment. Put the butter and sugar in a bowl, and whisk until pale and creamy. Add the lemon zest, and whisk slowly until well dispersed through the batter.

3 Beat in the eggs, a little at a time, mixing well after each addition to avoid curdling. Sift the flour into the batter and gently fold it in with a metal spoon, trying not to lose any air from the mixture. Finally, add the milk and gently and evenly mix it in.

4 Spread half the mixture in the prepared tin and smooth the surface with a palette knife. Arrange half the apple wedges over the batter, reserving the best pieces for the top. Spread the rest of the mixture over the apples. Smooth once more with a palette knife.

5 Arrange the remaining apple wedges on top of the cake. Remove the streusel dough from the fridge and coarsely grate it. Sprinkle the grated streusel evenly over the top of the cake.

6 Bake the cake in the centre of the oven for 45 minutes. Insert a skewer into the centre of the cake. If the skewer emerges coated in batter, cook for a few minutes more and test again. Leave the cake in the tin for 10 minutes to cool slightly. Keeping the streusel on top, remove the cake from the tin and cool on a wire rack. Serve warm.

Rich fruit cake

A wonderfully moist, rich cake. For large celebrations, bake in a square tin for easy portioning.

🥄 25 MINS, PLUS SOAKING

🍲 2 HRS 30 MINS

SPECIAL EQUIPMENT

25cm (10in) deep round cake tin

electric hand-held whisk

SERVES 16

200g (7oz) sultanas

400g (14oz) raisins

350g (12oz) prunes, chopped

350g (12oz) glacé cherries

2 apples, peeled, cored, and diced

600ml (1 pint) cider

4 tsp mixed spice

200g (7oz) unsalted butter, softened

175g (6oz) dark brown sugar

3 eggs, lightly beaten

150g (5½ oz) ground almonds

280g (10oz) plain flour, plus extra

for dusting

2 tsp baking powder

400g (14oz) ready-made marzipan

2–3 tbsp apricot jam

3 large egg whites

500g (1lb 2oz) icing sugar

1 Place the sultanas, raisins, prunes, cherries, apples, cider, and spice in a saucepan. Bring to a simmer over a medium-low heat, then cover for 20 minutes until most of the liquid is absorbed. Cover and leave overnight at room temperature so that the fruits absorb the remaining liquid.

2 Preheat the oven to 160°C (325°F/Gas 3). Double-line a 25cm (10in) deep round cake tin with baking parchment. With an electric hand-held whisk, cream the butter and sugar in a large

bowl until fluffy. Add the eggs, a little at a time, beating very well after each addition to avoid curdling.

3 Gently fold in the fruit mix and ground almonds, trying to keep volume in the batter. Sift the flour and baking powder into the bowl, then gently fold into the mixture. Spoon the batter into the prepared tin, cover with foil, and bake for 2½ hours.

4 Test the cake is ready: a skewer inserted into the centre should come out clean. Leave to cool, then turn out onto a wire rack to cool completely. Remove the baking parchment. Trim the cake to level it. Transfer to a stand and hold it in place with a small ball of marzipan.

5 Warm the jam and brush thickly over the whole cake.

This will help the marzipan stick. On a lightly floured surface, knead the remaining marzipan until softened. Roll out the softened marzipan until wide enough to cover the cake top and sides.

6 Drape the marzipan over the rolling pin and lift it over the cake. With your hands, gently ease the marzipan into place, smoothing out any bumps. With a small, sharp knife, cut away any excess marzipan from the base of the cake.

7 Place the egg whites in a bowl and sift in the icing sugar, stirring well to combine. With an electric hand-held whisk, beat for 10 minutes until stiff. Spread the icing neatly over the cake with a palette knife. Wipe the cake stand clean and leave the icing to set overnight before serving.

Lemon drizzle cake

The gloriously tangy lemon topping poured over the light sponge, produces a moist and mouthwatering cake.

🥄 **20 MINS**

🍲 **30 MINS**

❄️ **FREEZABLE**

SPECIAL EQUIPMENT

electric hand-held whisk

18cm (7in) round cake tin

SERVES 8

150g (5½oz) butter, softened

150g (5½oz) caster sugar

3 eggs

finely grated zest of 1 lemon

150g (5½oz) self-raising flour, sifted

FOR THE TOPPING

3 tbsp lemon juice

75g (2½oz) caster sugar

icing sugar, for dusting

1 Preheat the oven to 180°C (350°F/Gas 4). In a large bowl, cream together the butter and sugar with an electric hand-held whisk until light and fluffy. Whisk in the eggs one at a time, then add the zest.

2 Fold in the flour until just incorporated and pour the batter into a lined 18cm (7in) round cake tin. Bake in the centre of the preheated oven for 30 minutes until well risen and a skewer comes out clean.

3 To make the topping, gently heat the lemon juice and sugar in a small pan until the sugar has dissolved. Prick the cake all over with a thin wooden skewer and, leaving it in the tin, carefully pour the sugary mixture all over the top, a little at a time, until it has been absorbed. Allow the topping to cool before serving the cake, dusted with icing sugar.

Lemon curd cake

For a light and tasty alternative to buttercream filling, try this mix of mascarpone cheese with lemon curd instead.

🥄 25 MINS

🍲 20-25 MINS

❄️ FREEZABLE

SPECIAL EQUIPMENT

2 x 18cm (7in) cake tins

electric hand-held whisk

SERVES 8

175g (6oz) butter, softened, plus extra for greasing

175g (6oz) caster sugar

3 eggs, lightly beaten

175g (6oz) self-raising flour, sifted

1 tsp baking powder, sifted

finely grated zest and juice of 1 lemon

6 tbsp lemon curd

250g (9oz) mascarpone cheese

icing sugar, sifted, for dusting

1 Preheat the oven to 160°C (325°F/Gas 3). Grease two 18cm (7in) cake tins and line the bases with baking parchment.

2 Place the butter and sugar in a mixing bowl and cream them together using an electric hand-held whisk until pale and fluffy.

3 Gradually whisk in the eggs. Fold in the flour and baking powder, then the lemon zest and juice and 2 tbsp of the lemon curd.

4 Divide the mixture between the tins and level the surfaces with the back of a metal spoon.

5 Bake for 20–25 minutes, or until a skewer comes out clean. Leave in the tins for 10 minutes, then turn out onto a wire rack, remove the baking parchment, and allow to cool completely.

6 Place the mascarpone and remaining 4 tbsp of lemon curd in a bowl and stir together.

7 Place a cake on a serving plate and spread the filling over. Top with the remaining cake and dust evenly with icing sugar.

HOW TO FREEZE

Freeze the just-cooled cakes before filling, individually wrapped in cling film and sealed with foil, for up to 12 weeks. Defrost thoroughly, then fill the cakes from the start of step 6.

Lemon polenta cake

Polenta makes a rich, moist cake with a great lemon flavour. This recipe is also a good wheat-free option.

- 30 MINS
- 50-60 MINS
- FREEZABLE

SPECIAL EQUIPMENT

23cm (9in) round springform cake tin

electric hand whisk

SERVES 6-8

175g (6oz) unsalted butter, softened

200g (7oz) caster sugar

3 large eggs, beaten

75g (2½ oz) coarse yellow cornmeal or polenta

175g (6oz) ground almonds

grated zest and juice of 2 lemons

1 tsp baking powder

crème fraîche, to serve (optional)

1 Preheat the oven to 160°C (325°F/Gas 3). Grease the cake tin and line the base with baking parchment. Cream the butter and 175g (6oz) of the sugar with an electric hand whisk until fluffy. Pour in the beaten eggs, a little at a time, whisking after each addition.

Gently fold in the cornmeal or polenta and the almonds using a metal spoon. Fold in the lemon zest and baking powder.

2 Scrape the mixture into the prepared tin and smooth the surface with a palette knife. Bake for 50–60 minutes until springy to the touch and a skewer inserted in the centre comes out clean. It will not rise much. Leave the cake in the tin for a few minutes until cool enough to handle.

3 Heat the lemon juice and the remaining sugar in a small pan over a medium heat until the sugar has dissolved. Remove from the heat.

4 Turn the cake out onto a wire rack, baked side upwards. Retain the parchment. Using a thin skewer or cocktail stick, poke holes in the top of the cake while still warm. Pour the hot lemon syrup, a little at a time, over the surface of the cake. Remove the parchment and serve at room temperature on its own or with crème fraîche.

Chocolate orange pound cake

Candied orange peel adds great flavour to this loaf cake.

- 2 HRS
- 50-60 MINS

SPECIAL EQUIPMENT

900g (2lb) loaf tin

electric hand whisk

SERVES 6-8

125g (4½ oz) plain flour

3 tbsp cocoa powder

1 tsp baking powder

salt

175g (6oz) unsalted butter

200g (7oz) caster sugar

3 eggs

2 large pieces of candied orange peel, chopped, plus extra for decoration

60g (2oz) icing sugar

1 Preheat the oven to 180°C (350°F/Gas 4). Butter, line, and flour the loaf tin. Sift the flour into a bowl with the cocoa powder, baking powder, and a pinch of salt. In another bowl, cream the butter and sugar with an electric hand whisk until light and fluffy. Add the eggs, one by one, beating thoroughly after each addition. Stir in the chopped candied orange peel.

2 Lightly fold in the flour and cocoa mixture. Transfer the mixture to the prepared loaf tin. Tap the tin on a work surface to level the surface, and bake for 50–60 minutes, until it shrinks slightly from the sides of the tin and a skewer inserted in the centre comes out clean.

3 Run a knife around the sides of the tin to loosen the cake, invert the tin, and transfer the cake to a wire rack. Keep a baking sheet below the rack to catch any drips from the icing later. Remove the baking parchment. Leave the cake to cool completely.

4 Sift the icing sugar into a small bowl and slowly stir in enough of the orange juice to make a soft paste. Place the bowl in a saucepan of hot (not simmering) water and heat until the icing is warm and pours easily from the spoon. Drizzle the icing over the cake. Finely slice the reserved candied peel and use to top the cake. Leave to stand for about 1 hour, until the icing has set. Serve in slices.

Orange and rosemary polenta cake

Wonderfully moist, this is one of the few wheat-free cakes that work just as well as those made from wheat flour.

 30 MINS

🍲 50 MINS-1 HR

SPECIAL EQUIPMENT

23cm (9in) round springform cake tin

electric hand-held whisk

SERVES 6-8

juice and finely grated zest of 1 large orange

200g (7oz) caster sugar

sprig of rosemary

175g (6oz) unsalted butter, softened, plus extra for greasing

3 large eggs, lightly beaten

75g (2½ oz) coarse or fine polenta

175g (6oz) ground almonds

1 tsp gluten-free baking powder

crème fraîche, to serve (optional)

1 Put the orange juice and 25g (scant 1oz) of the sugar in a small pan. Heat over a medium heat, stirring from time to time, until the sugar has dissolved. Add the rosemary, remove from the heat, and leave to infuse.

2 Preheat the oven to 160°C (325°F/Gas 3). Grease a 23cm (9in) round springform cake tin, and line the base with baking parchment. With an electric hand-held whisk, cream the butter and remaining sugar until fluffy. Gradually add the eggs, a little at a time, whisking well after each addition. Add the polenta and

almonds, and gently fold in with a metal spoon. Finally, fold in the orange zest and baking powder. The batter will seem quite stiff.

3 Scrape the mixture into the prepared tin and smooth the surface with a palette knife. Bake the cake for 50–60 minutes; it will not rise much. Check the cake is cooked by inserting a skewer; it should come out clean. Leave the cake in the tin and reheat the orange and rosemary syrup over a medium heat until hot. Remove and discard the rosemary.

4 While the cake and syrup are both still hot, poke holes in the cake using a thin skewer or cocktail stick. Pour the syrup a little at a time over the cake. Pour

more on only once the syrup has soaked into the cake, until it is all used up. Once cooled, carefully remove the cake from the tin, remove the baking parchment, and serve at room temperature, with crème fraîche (if using). It will keep in an airtight container for up to 3 days.

HOW TO FREEZE

Wrap the just-cooled cake in baking parchment, then seal with foil. Freeze for up to 12 weeks. Defrost thoroughly before eating. If it has been previously frozen, this cake may benefit from reheating at 180°C (350°F/Gas 4) for 15 minutes before serving.

Chocolate orange truffle cake

Beneath the rich chocolate ganache topping lies a layer of chocolate sponge cake flavoured with Grand Marnier. Orange zest sprinkled over the top is the perfect finishing touch. Make sure you leave at least 6 hours' chilling time.

35-40 MINS PLUS CHILLING

40 MINS

SPECIAL EQUIPMENT

25cm (10in) round cake tin

electric hand whisk

23cm (9in) round springform cake tin

SERVES 10-12

100g (3½ oz) plain flour

30g (1oz) cocoa powder, plus 3 tbsp to decorate

salt

4 eggs

140g (5oz) caster sugar

60g (2oz) butter, melted and cooled

4-5 tbsp Grand Marnier

grated zest of 3 oranges

FOR THE CHOCOLATE GANACHE

375g (13oz) plain chocolate, cut into large chunks

375ml (13fl oz) double cream

3 tbsp Grand Marnier

1 Preheat the oven to 220°C (425°F/Gas 7). Butter the 25cm (10in) cake tin and line the bottom with baking parchment. Butter the parchment. Sprinkle in 2–3 tbsp flour, and turn the tin to coat the bottom and side; tap the tin upside down to remove excess flour.

2 Sift together the flour, cocoa powder, and a pinch of salt. Put the eggs in a large bowl and beat with an electric hand whisk for a few seconds. Add the sugar and continue beating for about 5 minutes, until the mixture leaves a ribbon trail when the beaters are lifted.

3 Sift about a third of the flour and cocoa mixture over the egg mixture and fold together. Add another third of the flour and cocoa mixture and fold together in the same way. Add the remaining flour and cocoa mixture and the butter, and fold them in gently, but quickly.

4 Pour the mixture into the prepared tin, then gently tap the tin on the work surface to level the mixture and knock out any large air bubbles. Bake for about 40 minutes, until the cake has risen and is just firm to the touch. Turn the cake out onto a wire rack. Peel off the paper and leave to cool.

5 Trim the cooled cake to fit the 23cm (9in) springform tin. Lightly butter the bottom and side. Transfer the trimmed cake to the tin. Sprinkle the Grand Marnier evenly over the top, cover, and set aside.

6 For the chocolate ganache, put the chocolate in a large bowl. Heat the cream until almost boiling, then pour it over the chocolate. Stir until the chocolate has melted. Allow to cool, stirring occasionally. Add the Grand Marnier and gently stir until blended. Using the electric hand whisk, beat the chocolate ganache for 5–10 minutes, until fluffy. Do not overbeat, or it will be very stiff. With a rubber spatula or a wooden spoon, turn out the chocolate ganache on top of the cake and smooth the surface. Cover with cling film and chill for at least 6 hours, until firm.

7 Just before serving, take the cake from the fridge. Stand it on top of a bowl, then release the side of the tin. Carefully remove the base of the tin, using a palette knife. Place the cake on a wire rack with a baking sheet beneath. Sift cocoa powder over the top, using a stencil if you like, then transfer to a serving plate and sprinkle with the orange zest.

Chocolate fudge cake

Everyone loves a good fudge cake, and this is a winner. The oil and syrup keep it moist, and the icing is a classic.

🥄 **40 MINS**

🍲 **30 MINS**

❄ **FREEZABLE**

SPECIAL EQUIPMENT

2 x 20cm (8in) round cake tins

electric hand-held whisk

SERVES 6-8

150ml (5fl oz) sunflower oil, plus extra for greasing

175g (6oz) self-raising flour

25g (scant 1oz) cocoa powder

1 tsp baking powder

150g (5½ oz) soft light brown sugar

3 tbsp golden syrup

2 eggs, lightly beaten

150ml (5fl oz) whole milk

FOR THE ICING

125g (4½ oz) unsalted butter

25g (scant 1oz) cocoa powder

125g (4½ oz) icing sugar

2 tbsp whole milk, if necessary

1 Preheat the oven to 180°C (350°F/Gas 4). Grease two 20cm (8in) round cake tins and line the bases with baking parchment. In a large bowl, sift together the flour, cocoa, and baking powder. Mix in the sugar.

2 Gently heat the golden syrup until runny and leave to cool. In a separate bowl, beat the eggs, oil, and milk together using an electric hand-held whisk. Whisk the egg mixture into the flour

mixture until well combined, but don't over-mix. Gently fold in the syrup, being careful not to knock out any air, and divide the batter evenly between the cake tins.

3 Bake the cakes in the middle of the oven for 30 minutes, or until springy to the touch, and a skewer comes out clean. Leave to cool slightly in the tins, then turn out onto a wire rack to cool completely.

4 To make the icing, melt the butter over a low heat. Stir in the cocoa powder and cook gently for 1–2 minutes, then leave to cool completely. Sift the icing sugar into a bowl.

5 Pour the melted butter and cocoa into the icing sugar

and beat together to combine. If the mixture seems a little dry, add the milk, 1 tbsp at a time, until the icing is smooth and glossy. Leave to cool for up to 30 minutes; it will thicken as it cools. When thick, use half the icing to fill the cake and the other half to top it.

COOK'S TIP

This firm, very tempting cake is a great base for all sorts of novelty children's birthday cakes. Chill it, then carve into shapes, or simply smother with icing and stick their favourite sweets all over the top and sides, to make a show-stopping centrepiece.

Devil's food cake

In this American classic, coffee enhances the richness of the chocolate, adding a lovely depth of flavour to the cake.

⊻ 30 MINS

◨ 30-35 MINS

❄ FREEZABLE

SPECIAL EQUIPMENT

2 x 20cm (8in) round cake tins

electric hand-held whisk

SERVES 8-10

100g (3½ oz) unsalted butter, softened, plus extra for greasing

275g (9½ oz) caster sugar

2 large eggs

200g (7oz) self-raising flour

75g (2½ oz) cocoa powder

1 tsp baking powder

1 tbsp coffee powder mixed with 120ml (4fl oz) boiling water, or 120ml (4fl oz) cooled espresso

120ml (4fl oz) whole milk

1 tsp vanilla extract

FOR THE ICING

125g (4½ oz) unsalted butter, cut into cubes

25g (scant 1oz) cocoa powder

125g (4½ oz) icing sugar, sifted

2-3 tbsp whole milk

dark or milk chocolate, for shaving

1 Preheat the oven to 180°C (350°F/Gas 4). Grease two 20cm (8in) round cake tins and line the bases with baking parchment. Using an electric hand-held whisk, cream together the butter and sugar until light and fluffy.

2 Beat in the eggs one at a time, whisking well after each addition. In a separate bowl, sift together the flour, cocoa powder, and baking powder. In another bowl, mix together the cooled coffee, milk, and vanilla extract.

3 Beat alternate spoonfuls of the dry and liquid ingredients into the cake batter. Once well blended, divide between the tins.

4 Bake for 30–35 minutes until the cakes are springy to the touch and a skewer comes out clean. Leave to cool in the tins for a few minutes, then turn out onto a wire rack to cool completely.

5 For the icing, melt the butter in a pan over a low heat. Add the cocoa powder and continue to cook for a minute or two, stirring frequently. Allow to cool slightly.

6 Sift in the icing sugar, beating thoroughly to combine. Blend in the milk, 1 tbsp at a time, until smooth and glossy. Allow to cool (it will thicken), then use half to sandwich the cakes together and the remainder to decorate the top and sides of the cake. Finally, use a vegetable peeler to create chocolate shavings and scatter them evenly over the top of the cake.

HOW TO FREEZE

Freeze the just-baked, cooled, and un-iced cakes, wrapped separately in greaseproof paper and sealed with foil, for up to 6 months, then defrost, ice, and serve.

Chocolate decadence with raspberry coulis

A tart raspberry coulis cuts through this deliciously rich cake.

🥣 30–40 MINS PLUS CHILLING

🍲 20 MINS

SPECIAL EQUIPMENT

food processor

electric hand whisk

23cm (9in) round springform tin

SERVES 8

500g (1lb 2oz) plain chocolate

150g (5½ oz) unsalted butter

6 eggs, separated

2 tbsp caster sugar

1 tbsp plain flour

750g (1lb 10oz) raspberries, plus more to serve

2–3 tbsp icing sugar

crème fraîche or whipped double cream, to serve

1 Preheat the oven to 200°C (400°F/Gas 6). Butter the tin and line with greaseproof paper. Coat the base and sides in 2 tbsp flour and tap out the excess. Pulse the chocolate coarsely into pieces in a food processor. Cut the butter into pieces and put in a heatproof bowl with the chocolate. Set over a pan of hot, but not simmering, water. Stir until melted and smooth. Let cool, stirring occasionally.

2 Beat the egg yolks into the cooled chocolate with a wooden spoon. Put the egg whites in a clean bowl and whisk until stiff peaks form. Add the sugar and continue whisking for about 20 seconds until glossy. Stir the flour into the chocolate mix, then fold in one-third of the egg whites to lighten it. Fold in the rest of the whisked egg whites in 2 batches, then transfer to the tin.

3 Bake for about 20 minutes until crusty on top. Let cool completely in the tin, then set on a wire rack. When cold, chill for 2 hours. Then remove from the tin and peel off the paper.

4 Blitz the raspberries in a food processor. Add icing sugar to taste, pulse briefly, then work the puréed raspberries through a sieve into a bowl to remove all the pips.

5 Using a serrated knife, cut the cake into 8 wedges. Set 1 wedge in the centre of each plate. Ladle a small pool of raspberry coulis onto each plate near the tip of the wedge of cake. Decorate each plate with a few whole raspberries and serve with crème fraîche or whipped double cream.

Blueberry upside-down cake

This is an unusual yet delicious way of turning a punnet of blueberries and a few storecupboard essentials into a quick and delicious dessert for a crowd.

🥣 15 MINS

🍲 40 MINS

SPECIAL EQUIPMENT

23cm (9in) round springform cake tin

electric hand whisk

SERVES 8–10

150g (5½ oz) unsalted butter, softened

150g (5½ oz) caster sugar

3 eggs

1 tsp vanilla extract

100g (3½ oz) self-raising flour

1 tsp baking powder

50g (1¾ oz) ground almonds

250g (9oz) blueberries

1 Preheat the oven to 180°C (350°F/Gas 4) and place a baking sheet inside to heat up. Grease the cake tin and line the base with baking parchment.

2 Cream together the butter and sugar using an electric hand whisk, until light and fluffy. Gradually beat in the eggs and vanilla extract, whisking well between each addition, until well combined. Sift together the flour and baking powder, add the ground almonds, and fold into the batter.

3 Tip the blueberries into the tin and spread the batter gently over them. Bake the cake on the baking sheet in the centre of the oven for 35–40 minutes until golden brown and springy to the touch; a skewer should come out clean when inserted in the centre. Leave the cake to cool for a few minutes, before removing from the tin.

4 Place the cake on a serving plate. Serve warm as a dessert, topped with cream or light vanilla custard; or serve cold, dusted with icing sugar.

Cherry and almond cake

A classic combination of flavours and a traditional cake that is always popular with guests.

🥄 20 MINS

🍲 1 HR 30 MINS-1 HR 45 MINS

❄️ FREEZABLE

SPECIAL EQUIPMENT

20cm (8in) round deep springform cake tin

electric hand whisk or mixer

SERVES 8-10

150g (5½ oz) unsalted butter, softened

150g (5½ oz) caster sugar

2 large eggs, lightly beaten

250g (9oz) self-raising flour, sifted

1 tsp baking powder

150g (5½ oz) ground almonds

1 tsp vanilla extract

75ml (2½ fl oz) whole milk

400g (14oz) cherries, stoned

25g (scant 1oz) blanched almonds, chopped

1 Preheat the oven to 180°C (350°F/Gas 4). Grease the tin and line the base with baking parchment. Put the butter and sugar in a mixing bowl and whisk with an electric hand whisk or mixer until pale and creamy. Whisk in the eggs one at a time, adding 1 tbsp of flour to the mixture before adding the second egg.

2 Mix in the remaining flour, baking powder, ground almonds, vanilla extract, and milk. Mix in half the cherries, then spoon the mixture into the tin and smooth the top. Scatter the remaining cherries and all the almonds over the surface.

3 Bake for 1½–1¾ hours, or until golden brown and firm to the touch. A skewer inserted into the centre should come out clean. If the surface of the cake starts to brown before it is fully cooked, cover with foil. When cooked, leave to cool in the tin for a few minutes, then remove the foil and parchment, and transfer to a wire rack to cool completely before serving.

Tropical angel cake

Pineapple and mango crown a deliciously tasty coconut cake.

🥄 15 MINS

🍲 30 MINS

SPECI AL EQUIPMENT

electric hand whisk or mixer

1.2 x 1.5-litre (2 x 2¾-pints) savarin ring mould

SERVES 6-8

FOR THE CAKE

4 large egg whites

½ tsp cream of tartar

150g (5½ oz) caster sugar

50g (1¾ oz) plain flour

10g (¼ oz) cornflour

25g (scant 1oz) desiccated coconut

FOR THE TOPPING

200g (7oz) Greek-style yogurt

200g (7oz) mixed peeled and chopped tropical fruit, such as pineapple and mango

seeds and pulp from 2 passion fruits

lime zest, to decorate

1 Preheat the oven to 190°C (375°F/Gas 5). Put the egg whites, cream of tartar, and 1 tbsp cold water in a large mixing bowl and whisk with an electric whisk or mixer until stiff peaks form. Whisk in 1 tbsp sugar at a time until the mix is stiff and shiny.

2 Sift in the flour and cornflour and gently fold them in together with the coconut until well combined. Carefully spoon the mixture into the ring mould and smooth the top, pressing down gently so there are no air pockets left. Bake in the oven for 15 minutes, then reduce the oven temperature to 180°C (350°F/Gas 4) and bake for a further 15 minutes until the cake is firm to the touch and golden brown.

3 Place the ring mould upside-down on a wire rack and leave until completely cold, then carefully ease the cake out of the mould with a round-bladed knife or small metal spatula and place on a serving plate.

4 To make the topping, beat the yogurt lightly so it is smooth and creamy, then spoon it into the centre of the cake. Top it with the tropical fruit, then drizzle the passion fruit seeds and pulp over the top. Finish by scattering over the lime zest.

Red grape and cinnamon cakes

Eat this delightful cake warm as a dessert with cream, yogurt, or custard, or cold with a cup of coffee. The grapes turn into a layer of sticky fruit on top of the cake and keep it moist.

🥣 **30 MINS**

🍲 **50 MINS**

SPECIAL EQUIPMENT

20cm (8in) round springform cake tin

blender or food processor

SERVES 6-8

300g (10oz) red grapes, halved lengthways

2 tbsp light soft brown sugar

150g (5½ oz) caster sugar

150g (5½ oz) butter, softened

3 eggs

½ tsp vanilla extract

150g (5½ oz) self-raising flour

1 tsp ground cinnamon

1 heaped tsp baking powder

1 Preheat the oven to 180°C (350°F/Gas 4). Line the cake tin with greaseproof paper. Spread the grapes evenly, skin-side down, on the bottom of the cake tin and scatter the brown sugar over the top.

2 Put the caster sugar and butter in a blender or food processor and blitz. When the mixture is smooth, add the eggs and vanilla extract and pulse to mix well. Add the flour, cinnamon, and baking powder and pulse the mixture again briefly until it is blended.

3 Spread the sponge mixture over the grapes. Place the cake tin on a baking tray and bake in the centre of the oven for approximately 50 minutes until risen and golden brown and a skewer through the middle comes out clean. Turn the cake out onto a serving plate, carefully peeling off the greaseproof paper to reveal the grape topping. Serve warm or cold.

Courgette cake

This intriguing alternative to carrot cake makes an unusual use of courgettes when they are at their most plentiful.

🥣 **20 MINS**

🍲 **45 MINS**

❄️ **FREEZABLE**

SPECIAL EQUIPMENT

23cm (9in) round springform cake tin

SERVES 8-10

100g (3½ oz) hazelnuts

225ml (7½ fl oz) sunflower oil

3 large eggs

1 tsp vanilla extract

225g (8oz) caster sugar

200g (7oz) courgettes, grated

200g (7oz) self-raising flour

75g (2½ oz) wholemeal self-raising flour

pinch of salt

1 tsp cinnamon

grated zest of 1 lemon

1 Preheat the oven to 180°C (350°F/Gas 4). Oil the base and sides of the tin and line the base with baking parchment. Spread the hazelnuts on a baking tray and cook for 5 minutes until lightly browned. Put the nuts on a clean tea towel and rub them to get rid of any excess skin. Roughly chop and set aside.

2 Pour the oil and eggs into a bowl, then add the vanilla and sugar. Whisk the oil mixture until lighter in colour and thickened. Squeeze moisture from the courgettes and fold in with the nuts. Sift over the flour. Add the salt, cinnamon, and lemon zest, and fold.

3 Pour the batter into the tin. Bake for 45 minutes, or until springy to the touch. Turn out onto a wire rack to cool completely.

Cinnamon apple cake

This recipe is rather like making a sweet toad-in-the-hole. It can be served warm as a dessert with custard or cream, or left to cool and sliced to serve with coffee.

🥣 30 MINS
🍲 25-30 MINS

SPECIAL EQUIPMENT

electric hand whisk

24cm (9½ in) large square baking tin

SERVES 8-12

3-4 cooking apples (depending on size)

1 tbsp lemon juice

3 eggs

250g (9oz) caster sugar

115g (4oz) butter, diced

6 tbsp milk

4 tbsp single cream

200g (7oz) plain flour

1 tbsp baking powder

2 tsp ground cinnamon

1 Preheat the oven to 200°C (400°F/Gas 6). Butter a large baking tin, about 24cm (9½ in) square, and dust with flour.

2 Peel, core, quarter, and slice the apples, and put in a bowl of water with lemon juice to prevent browning.

3 Whisk the eggs and 225g (8oz) of the sugar with an electric hand whisk until thick and pale, and leaves a trail when the beaters are lifted out of the mixture.

4 Put the butter, milk, and cream in a pan and heat gently until the butter melts, then bring to the boil. Remove the pan from the heat and allow to cool briefly, then stir into the egg mixture. Sift the flour and baking powder over the surface, and fold in with a metal spoon. Pour into the prepared tin.

5 Drain the apples and arrange them attractively over the batter. Mix the remaining sugar with the cinnamon, and sprinkle over. Bake for 25–30 minutes until golden and cooked through. Leave to cool in the tin, then cut into squares.

Apple, sultana, and pecan cake

If you like a healthier cake, this is an excellent choice. It uses little fat and is packed full of fruit and nuts, making it a wholesome yet delicious choice.

🥣 25 MINS
🍲 30-35 MINS

SPECIAL EQUIPMENT

23cm (9in) round springform cake tin

SERVES 10-12

50g (1¾ oz) shelled pecan nuts

200g (7oz) apples, peeled, cored, and finely diced

150g (5½ oz) light soft brown sugar

250g (9oz) self-raising flour

1 tsp baking powder

2 tsp cinnamon

salt

3½ tbsp sunflower oil

3½ tbsp milk

2 eggs

1 tsp vanilla extract

50g (1¾ oz) sultanas

whipped cream or icing sugar, to serve (optional)

1 Preheat the oven to 180°C (350°F/Gas 4). Grease the cake tin with butter and line the base with baking parchment. Place the nuts on a baking sheet and toast them in the oven for 5 minutes until crisp. Allow to cool, then roughly chop.

2 Mix the apples and sugar together in a large mixing bowl. Sift over the flour, baking powder, cinnamon, and a little salt, and fold in. Then whisk together the oil, milk, eggs, and vanilla extract in a jug.

3 Pour the milk into the cake mixture and stir until well combined. Fold in the pecans and sultanas, and pour the mixture into the prepared tin.

4 Bake in the centre of the oven for 30–35 minutes until a skewer comes out clean. Leave to cool for a few minutes in the tin, then turn out onto a wire rack and remove the baking parchment. Serve warm with whipped cream as a dessert, or cooled and dusted with icing sugar.

Vanilla cupcakes with vanilla frosting

Cupcakes are an easy treat to bake, and are fabulous when freshly made. They're easy to whip up in a hurry, too.

🥄 25 MINS

🍲 16–18 MINS

❄️ FREEZABLE

SPECIAL EQUIPMENT

electric hand-held whisk

12-hole muffin tin

12 cupcake cases

piping bag and star nozzle (optional)

MAKES 12

100g (3½ oz) butter, softened

150g (5½ oz) caster sugar

3 eggs, lightly beaten

1 tsp vanilla extract

200g (7oz) self-raising flour

1 tsp baking powder

3½ tbsp milk, plus 1 tbsp if needed

FOR THE BUTTERCREAM

200g (7oz) icing sugar

100g (3½ oz) butter, softened

1 tsp vanilla extract

1 Preheat the oven to 180°C (350°F/Gas 4). Place the butter and sugar in a large bowl, and use an electric hand-held whisk to cream them together until the mixture is very light and fluffy. Whisk in the eggs and vanilla extract until they are well combined.

2 Sift together the flour and baking powder. Add one-third of the flour to the cake batter and whisk it in well. Add half of the milk and whisk it again, then another one-third of the flour, the rest of the milk, and finally the last one-third of the flour, making sure to whisk well between each addition.

3 Place 12 cupcake cases in a deep 12-hole muffin tin (this will help the cupcakes keep their shape on cooking). Carefully spoon the cake mixture into the cases, filling each two-thirds full.

4 Bake for 16–18 minutes, until lightly coloured, firm, and springy to the touch, and a toothpick inserted into the centre of a cupcake comes out clean. Do not be tempted to open the oven until at least 15 minutes baking time has passed. Transfer the cupcakes to a wire rack to cool.

5 To make the buttercream, beat the icing sugar, butter, and vanilla until smooth, light, and creamy, adding up to 1 tbsp milk, if needed, for a piping consistency, and transfer it to a piping bag fitted with a star-shaped nozzle (if using).

6 When the cakes are completely cold, they are ready to ice. Ice them by hand using the back of a spoon dipped in warm water to smooth the surface of the frosting, or pipe the buttercream onto the cupcakes.

Red velvet cupcakes with cream cheese icing

These fashionable cupcakes taste as good as they look, with red-toned cake against pale buttery icing.

🥄 25 MINS

🍲 22-25 MINS

❄ FREEZABLE

SPECIAL EQUIPMENT

electric hand-held whisk

18-20 cupcake cases

2 x 12-hole muffin tins

piping bag and star nozzle (optional)

MAKES 18-20

125g (4½ oz) butter, softened

250g (9oz) caster sugar

2 eggs, lightly beaten

2 tsp red food colouring

1 tsp vanilla extract

250g (9oz) self-raising flour

4 tbsp cocoa powder

200ml (7fl oz) buttermilk

1 tsp cider vinegar

1 tsp bicarbonate of soda

FOR THE ICING

50g (1¾ oz) cream cheese

50g (1¾ oz) butter, softened

200g (7oz) icing sugar

1 tsp vanilla extract

1 Preheat the oven to 180°C (350°F/Gas 4). Place the butter and sugar in a large bowl, and use an electric hand-held whisk to cream them together until the mixture is very light and fluffy. Whisk in the eggs, food colouring, and vanilla extract until they are well combined.

2 Sift together the flour and cocoa powder. Add one-third of the flour to the cake batter and whisk it in well. Add half of the buttermilk and whisk it again, then another one-third of the flour, the rest of the buttermilk, and the final one-third of the flour, making sure to whisk well between additions. Mix together the cider vinegar and bicarbonate of soda and fold quickly into the batter.

3 Place 18–20 cupcake cases in 2 deep 12-hole muffin tins (they will help the cupcakes keep their shape). Spoon the batter into the cases, filling each two-thirds full. Bake for 22–25 minutes, until springy to the touch. Do not open the oven until at least 20 minutes baking time has passed. Transfer to a wire rack to cool.

4 To make the icing, beat the cream cheese, butter, icing sugar, and vanilla extract until light and creamy, and transfer to a piping bag fitted with a star-shaped nozzle (if using).

5 When the cakes are completely cold, they are ready to ice. Ice them by hand using the back of a spoon dipped in warm water to smooth the surface, or pipe the icing onto the cupcakes.

PREPARE AHEAD

The cupcakes can be made up to 1 day ahead and stored, un-iced, in an airtight container. They are best iced on the day they are to be eaten.

HOW TO FREEZE

The un-iced cupcakes can be frozen in an airtight container for up to 12 weeks. Defrost thoroughly before icing.

Angel food cake

This American classic is named for its pure white, light-as-air fat-free sponge. It is best eaten on the day it is made.

30 MINS

35–45 MINS

SPECIAL EQUIPMENT

1.7-litre (3-pint) ring mould

sugar thermometer (optional)

SERVES 8–12

large knob of butter, for greasing

150g (5½ oz) plain flour, sifted

100g (3½ oz) icing sugar, sifted, plus extra for dusting

8 egg whites (keep the yolks for custards and tart fillings)

pinch of cream of tartar

250g (9oz) caster sugar

few drops of almond or vanilla extract

FOR THE FROSTING

150g (5½ oz) caster sugar

2 egg whites

strawberries (halved), blueberries, and raspberries, to decorate

1 Preheat the oven to 180°C (350°F/Gas 4). Melt the butter in a small pan and use generously to brush the inside of a 1.7-litre (3-pint) ring mould. Sift the flour and icing sugar, again, into a bowl.

2 Whisk the egg whites and cream of tartar until stiff, then whisk in the caster sugar, 1 tbsp at a time. Sift the flour mixture into the egg white mixture and fold it in with a metal spoon, then fold in the almond or vanilla extract.

3 Spoon the mixture gently into the ring mould, filling right to the brim, and level the surface with a palette knife. Place the mould on a baking tray and bake for 35–45 minutes, or until just firm to the touch.

4 Carefully remove the cake from the oven and invert the mould onto a wire rack. Leave the cake to cool, then ease it out of the mould.

5 To make the frosting, place the caster sugar in a saucepan with 4 tbsp of water. Heat gently, stirring, until the sugar dissolves. Now increase the heat and boil until the syrup reaches "soft-ball" stage (114–118°C/238–245°F) on a sugar thermometer, or until a little

of the syrup forms a soft ball when dropped into very cold water.

6 Meanwhile, whisk the egg whites until stiff. As soon as the sugar syrup reaches the correct temperature, plunge the base of the pan into a sink of cold water to stop the syrup getting any hotter. Slowly pour the syrup into the egg whites, whisking constantly. Keep whisking for 5 minutes, or until stiff peaks form.

7 Working quickly, because the frosting will set, spread it thinly all over the inside and outside of the cake with a palette knife, swirling the surface to create texture. Top with strawberries, blueberries, and raspberries, and sift over icing sugar to serve.

Cheesy bacon and spring onion muffins

Spring onions have a milder taste than onion, so they are a perfect addition to these light savoury muffins.

🥣 **15 MINS**

🍲 **25 MINS**

❄️ **FREEZABLE**

SPECIAL EQUIPMENT

4 x 150ml (5fl oz) metal pudding moulds or ramekins

SERVES 4

150g (5½ oz) back bacon rashers

200g (7oz) Cheddar cheese, cut into small pieces

125g (4½ oz) fresh breadcrumbs

4 spring onions, trimmed and finely chopped

3 eggs

100ml (3½ fl oz) milk

handful of chives, chopped

salt and freshly ground black pepper

1 Preheat the oven to 190°C (375°F/Gas 5). Fry the bacon rashers in a non-stick frying pan over a medium-high heat until they are cooked but not too crispy. Then cut the bacon into bite-sized pieces with a pair of kitchen scissors.

2 Place the Cheddar cheese, breadcrumbs, spring onions, eggs, and milk in a bowl and mix them together. Add the bacon and chives, stir them into the mixture, and season with salt and pepper.

3 Spoon the mixture into non-stick or greased pudding moulds or ramekins and bake in the oven for about 25 minutes until risen and golden.

Banana cake

Leftover bananas deteriorate rapidly. Use them up in this lovely moist cake that keeps for a couple of days.

🥣 **20 MINS**

🍲 **30 MINS, PLUS RESTING**

❄️ **FREEZABLE**

SPECIAL EQUIPMENT

18cm (7in) square cake tin

electric hand-held whisk

SERVES 8

150g (5½ oz) unsalted butter, softened, plus extra for greasing

150g (5½ oz) caster sugar

3 eggs

1 tsp vanilla extract

2 over-ripe bananas, peeled and mashed

150g (5½ oz) self-raising flour

½ tsp ground cinnamon

1 Preheat the oven to 180°C (350°F/Gas 4). Grease an 18cm (7in) square cake tin and line the base with baking parchment.

2 In a large bowl, beat the butter and sugar together with an electric hand-held whisk until light and fluffy. Whisk in the eggs, one at a time, until they are well mixed. Whisk in the vanilla extract.

3 Fold the mashed banana into the mixture until it is well combined. Sift the flour and cinnamon into the mixture and gently fold in.

4 Pour the batter into the tin and bake in the centre of the hot oven for 30 minutes. Remove the cake from the oven and allow it to rest in the tin for 5 minutes before removing it and allowing it to cool completely on a wire rack.

HOW TO FREEZE

The just-cooked and cooled cake can be wrapped well and frozen on the day it is made, for up to 12 weeks.

Banana and oatmeal muffins

These muffins are a tasty and healthy choice for a late leisurely brunch; delicious eaten when they're still warm.

20 MINS

30 MINS

❄ FREEZABLE

SPECIAL EQUIPMENT

12 paper muffin cases and/or 12-hole muffin tin

electric hand-held whisk

MAKES 12

110g (3¾ oz) butter, softened, plus extra for greasing (if using a tin)

160g (5¾ oz) plain flour

1 tsp bicarbonate of soda

1 tsp baking powder

1 tsp ground cinnamon

100g (3½ oz) oatmeal

50g (1¾ oz) chopped walnuts (optional)

100g (3½ oz) demerara sugar

2 eggs, lightly beaten

3 ripe bananas, mashed

120ml (4fl oz) whole milkt

1 Preheat the oven to 190°C (375°F/Gas 5). Place 12 paper muffin cases in a 12-hole muffin tin, or simply place the cases on a baking tray, or grease a 12-hole muffin tin with butter.

2 Sift the flour, bicarbonate of soda, baking powder, cinnamon, and oatmeal into a large bowl. Tip in any bran left in the sieve. Add the walnuts (if using). Stir well.

3 Place the butter and demerara sugar in a separate mixing bowl and cream together, using an electric hand-held whisk, until very light and fluffy. (This could take as much as 5 minutes, so be patient!) Add the eggs and mix well. Stir in the bananas and milk.

4 Pour the wet mixture into the dry and stir to combine. Do not over-mix or the muffins will be heavy. Divide the mixture between the paper cases or muffin tin holes.

5 Bake for 20 minutes (start checking after 15), or until a cocktail stick inserted into a muffin comes out clean. Transfer to a wire rack to cool.

HOW TO FREEZE

As soon as the muffins have cooled, open-freeze them on a baking sheet. When they are frozen solid (after about 3 hours), transfer them to a large freezer bag and seal. This way you can remove and defrost only as many as you need, and they won't turn stale.

Banana, date, and walnut loaf

This classic combination of flavours is the perfect mix of sweet and mellow. Just right for teatime.

🥣 **20 MINS**

🍲 **1-1 HR 15MINS**

❄ **FREEZABLE**

SPECIAL EQUIPMENT

900g (2lb) loaf tin

electric hand-held whisk

SERVES 8-10

100g (3½ oz) butter, softened

100g (3½ oz) caster sugar

2 large eggs

225g (8oz) self-raising flour, sifted

2 bananas, approx. 300g (10oz) in total

100g (3½ oz) stoned dates (medjool are best), chopped

50g (1¾ oz) walnut pieces, roughly chopped

1 tsp baking powder

1 Preheat the oven to 180°C (350°F/Gas 4). Line a 900g (2lb) loaf tin with baking parchment. In a bowl, beat the butter and sugar with an electric hand-held whisk until pale, light, and fluffy. Add the eggs one at a time, beating well as you do so, and adding 1 tbsp of the flour after each to prevent the mixture from curdling.

2 Peel and mash the bananas in a small bowl with a fork, then stir into the loaf mixture, along with the chopped dates and walnuts. Fold in the remaining flour and the baking powder, then spoon the mixture into the tin. Smooth the top, pressing well into the corners.

3 Bake for 1–1¼ hours, or until risen and firm to the touch. If the top of the cake starts to brown too much before it is fully cooked, cover with foil. Leave to cool in the tin, then cut into slices.

Banana and date mini muffins

These delicious little cakes are sweetened with banana and dates to make a healthier treat.

 15 MINS

🍲 **12-15 MINS**

❄ **FREEZABLE**

SPECIAL EQUIPMENT

24 mini muffin cases

24-hole mini muffin tray

MAKES 20-24

50g (1¾ oz) plain flour

35g (1¼ oz) wholemeal flour

½ tsp bicarbonate of soda

½ tsp baking powder

½ tsp ground cinnamon

50g (1¾ oz) ready-to-eat soft dates, finely chopped

50g (1¾ oz) soft light brown sugar

1 small egg, lightly beaten

2 tbsp sunflower oil

1 ripe banana, mashed with a fork

1 Preheat the oven to 180°C (350°F/Gas 4). Place 24 mini paper muffin cases into a 24-hole mini muffin tray.

2 Sift the flours, bicarbonate of soda, baking powder, and cinnamon into a large mixing bowl. Add the dates and sugar and stir to mix well.

3 Stir together the egg and oil with a fork, and stir in the mashed banana. Pour the wet mixture into the dry and stir well to combine. Divide the batter evenly between the cases.

4 Bake in the centre of the oven for 12–15 minutes, or until a cocktail stick inserted into the centre of a muffin comes out clean. Transfer to a wire rack to cool.

Blueberry muffins with streusel topping

These muffins make a quick and easy anytime treat. Use frozen blueberries if you have them.

🥣 **20 MINS**

🍲 **15–20 MINS**

❄️ **FREEZABLE**

SPECIAL EQUIPMENT

12-hole muffin tin

12 paper muffin case

MAKES 12

FOR THE STREUSEL TOPPING

75g (2½ oz) soft light brown sugar

75g (2½ oz) plain flour

1 tsp ground cinnamon

25g (scant 1oz) butter

FOR THE MUFFINS

250g (9oz) self-raising flour

1 tsp baking powder

¼ tsp salt

125g (4½ oz) caster sugar

100ml (3½ fl oz) whole milk

100ml (3½ fl oz) plain yogurt

3½ tbsp sunflower oil

1 large egg, lightly beaten

1 tsp vanilla extract

100g (3½ oz) blueberries

1 Preheat the oven to 200°C (400°F/Gas 6) and line a 12-hole muffin tin with paper muffin cases. Make the topping: rub together the sugar, flour, cinnamon, and butter.

2 Sift the flour, baking powder, and salt into a bowl. Add the sugar. Measure the milk, yogurt, and oil into a jug, and beat in the egg and vanilla. Stir the wet ingredients into the dry, then mix in the berries. Spoon into the cases and top evenly with the streusel.

3 Bake for 15–20 minutes, cool in the tin for 5 minutes, then transfer to a wire rack to cool.

HOW TO FREEZE

The cooked muffins can be frozen in an airtight container for up to 6 months. Defrost thoroughly before serving.

Double chocolate chip muffins

These muffins make a quick after-school filler, or a great snack at any time of day.

🥣 **10 MINS**

🍲 **15 MINS**

❄️ **FREEZABLE**

SPECIAL EQUIPMENT

12 muffin cases

12-hole muffin tin

MAKES 12

225g (8oz) self-raising flour

1 tsp baking powder

50g (1¾ oz) cocoa powder

¼ tsp salt

125g (4½ oz) caster sugar

200ml (7fl oz) whole milk

75ml (2½ fl oz) sunflower oil

1 egg, lightly beaten

1 tsp vanilla extract

75g (2½ oz) chocolate chips

1 Preheat the oven to 200°C (400°F/Gas 6). Sift the flour, baking powder, cocoa powder, and salt into a large bowl. Use a balloon whisk to mix in the sugar.

2 Measure the milk and sunflower oil into a jug, then add the egg and vanilla extract and beat it all together thoroughly.

3 Pour the liquid into the centre of the dry ingredients, and mix with a wooden spoon until just amalgamated. Be careful not to over-mix. Fold through the chocolate chips.

4 Put 12 muffin cases into a 12-hole muffin tin, then divide the mixture equally between the cases. Bake in the middle of the preheated oven for 15 minutes, until well risen. Remove from the oven and allow the muffins to cool in the tin for 5 minutes before transferring to a wire rack to cool completely.

Lemon and poppy seed muffins

These light and lemony muffins make a pleasant, refreshing change when baked for weekend breakfast or brunch.

10 MINS

15 MINS

FREEZABLE

SPECIAL EQUIPMENT

12-hole muffin tin

12 paper muffin cases

MAKES 12

250g (9oz) self-raising flour

1 tsp baking powder

¼ tsp salt

125g (4½ oz) caster sugar

finely grated zest of 1 lemon

1 heaped tsp poppy seeds

100ml (3½ fl oz) whole milk

100ml (3½ fl oz) plain yogurt

3½ tbsp sunflower oil

1 large egg, lightly beaten

2 tbsp lemon juice

FOR THE GLAZE

2 tbsp lemon juice

150g (5½ oz) icing sugar

finely grated zest of 1 lemon

1 Preheat the oven to 200°C (400°F/Gas 6) and line a 12-hole muffin tin with paper muffin cases.

Sift the flour, baking powder, and salt into a large bowl. Use a balloon whisk to mix through the sugar, lemon zest, and poppy seeds.

2 Measure the milk, yogurt, and oil into a jug, then add the egg and lemon juice and beat it all together thoroughly. Pour the liquid into the centre of the dry ingredients and mix with a wooden spoon until just amalgamated. Be careful not to over-mix.

3 Divide the mixture equally between the muffin cases and bake in the middle of the preheated oven for 15 minutes until the muffins are lightly brown and well risen. Remove from the oven and allow them to cool in the tin for 5 minutes before transferring to a wire rack to cool completely.

4 For the glaze, mix the lemon juice and icing sugar to a thin icing, drizzle it over the muffins, and sprinkle them with lemon zest.

HOW TO FREEZE

The cooked muffins can be frozen in an airtight container for up to 6 months. Defrost thoroughly before serving.

Coconut and lime drizzle loaf

Add a tropical twist to your baking with this zesty coconut and lime cake.

🥣 **15 MINS, PLUS COOLING**

🍲 **45–50 MINS**

❄️ **FREEZABLE**

SPECIAL EQUIPMENT

900g (2lb) loaf tin

electric hand-held whiskn

SERVES 8–10

FOR THE CAKE

200g (7oz) unsalted butter, softened, plus extra for greasing

200g (7oz) caster sugar

4 eggs

200g (7oz) self-raising flour, sifted

75g (2½ oz) desiccated coconut

finely grated zest of 2 limes, plus juice of 1 lime

FOR THE TOPPING

juice of 2 limes

80g (2¾ oz) golden caster sugar

1 tbsp desiccated coconut

1 Preheat the oven to 160°C (325°F/Gas 3). Grease a 900g (2lb) loaf tin and line the base with baking parchment.

2 Place the butter and sugar in a bowl and cream together using an electric hand-held whisk until fluffy. Whisk in the eggs, one at a time. Fold in the flour, coconut, lime zest, and juice.

3 Transfer to the tin and level the surface with the back of a spoon. Bake for 45–50 minutes, or until a skewer comes out clean.

4 Meanwhile, for the topping, stir the lime juice and golden caster sugar in a small bowl.

5 Remove the cake from the oven and place it, in the tin, on a wire rack. With a skewer, make holes in the cake and pour the lime mixture over. Sprinkle with the coconut. Leave until completely cold. Remove from the tin, peel off the parchment, and serve.

Pecan and cranberry loaf

Dried cranberries are a novel alternative to the more usual raisins, adding sweet, sharp notes to this cake.

🥣 **30 MINS**

🍲 **50–60 MINS**

❄️ **FREEZABLE**

SPECIAL EQUIPMENT

900g (2lb) loaf tin

electric hand whisk

SERVES 8–10

100g (3½ oz) unsalted butter, plus extra for greasing

100g (3½ oz) soft light brown sugar

75g (2½ oz) dried cranberries, roughly chopped

50g (1¾ oz) pecans, roughly chopped

finely grated zest of 2 oranges and juice of up to 1 orange

2 eggs, lightly beaten

120ml (4fl oz) whole milk

225g (8oz) self-raising flour

½ tsp baking powder

½ tsp ground cinnamon

100g (3½ oz) icing sugar, sifted

1 Preheat the oven to 180°C (350°F/Gas 4). Grease a 900g (2lb) loaf tin and line with baking parchment. In a pan, melt the butter. Leave to cool slightly, then stir in the sugar, cranberries, pecans, and zest of 1 orange. Whisk together the eggs and milk, then stir them in.

2 In a separate bowl, sift together the flour, baking powder, and cinnamon. Fold into the batter, mixing well. Tip into the tin. Bake in the centre of the oven for 50–60 minutes. Leave to cool slightly, then turn out.

3 Mix the icing sugar and remaining orange zest. Add enough orange juice for a drizzling consistency. Drizzle over the cooled cake and leave to dry before slicing. This cake will store in an airtight container for up to 3 days.

Apricot and almond tray bake

This delicious tray bake is equally good served warm with Creamy custard or cold at teatime.

🥣 20 MINS

🍲 35–40 MINS

❄ FREEZABLE

SPECIAL EQUIPMENT

23cm (9in) square baking tin

electric hand-held whisk

MAKES 25 SQUARES

210g (7¼ oz) butter, softened, plus extra for greasing

210g (7¼ oz) granulated sugar

2 eggs, lightly beaten

2 tbsp milk

125g (4½ oz) self-raising flour

85g (3oz) ground almonds

100g (3½ oz) dried apricots, finely chopped

50g (1¾ oz) toasted flaked almonds

1 Preheat the oven to 160°C (325°F/Gas 3). Grease a 23cm (9in) square baking tin and line the base with baking parchment.

2 Place the butter and sugar in a bowl and cream together using an electric hand-held whisk, until pale and fluffy. Beat in the eggs and milk. Sift the flour into the bowl and fold into the mixture with the ground almonds.

3 Stir in the apricots and transfer to the prepared tin. Level the surface with the back of a metal serving spoon and sprinkle over the flaked almonds, pressing any loose nuts into the mixture. Bake for 35–40 minutes, or until a skewer comes out clean.

4 Remove from the oven and leave to cool in the tin for 10 minutes. Transfer to a wire rack to cool completely. Cut into 25 squares to serve.

Orange and marmalade loaf cake

The aroma of cinnamon, oranges, and marmalade fills the kitchen while this cake is in the oven.

🥣 15 MINS

🍲 45–50 MINS

❄ FREEZABLE

SPECIAL EQUIPMENT

900g (2lb) loaf tin

food processor

SERVES 8–10

100g (3½ oz) butter, cut into cubes, plus extra for greasing

225g (8oz) self-raising flour, sifted

1 tsp ground cinnamon

100g (3½ oz) golden caster sugar

finely grated zest of 2 oranges, plus juice of 1 orange

150g (5½ oz) marmalade

100ml (3½ fl oz) whole milk

125g (4½ oz) icing sugar, sifted

1 Preheat the oven to 180°C (350°F/Gas 4). Grease a 900g (2lb) loaf tin and line it with baking parchment.

2 Place the flour and cinnamon into a food processor with the butter. Process until the mixture resembles coarse breadcrumbs. Stir in the caster sugar.

3 Stir in the zest of 1 orange and all but 2 tbsp of the orange juice. Stir in all the marmalade and milk. Spoon the mixture into the prepared tin and bake for 45–50 minutes, or until a skewer comes out clean. Remove from the oven and cool in the tin for 5 minutes.

4 Turn the cake onto a wire rack, remove the baking parchment, and allow to cool completely.

5 Mix the reserved orange juice into the icing sugar 1 tbsp at a time; you probably won't need it all. When it has reached a consistency you like, drizzle it over the cake. Sprinkle the reserved orange zest over (this looks more attractive if you use a zesting tool, rather than a box grater), and set aside for the icing to set.

Strawberries and cream whoopie pies

Best served immediately, these strawberry layered pies make a lovely addition to a traditional afternoon tea.

🥣 **40 MINS**

🍲 **12 MINS**

❄️ **FREEZABLE**

MAKES 10

175g (6oz) unsalted butter, softened

150g (5½ oz) soft light brown sugar

1 large egg, lightly beaten

1 tsp vanilla extract

225g (8oz) self-raising flour

75g (2½ oz) cocoa powder

1 tsp baking powder

150ml (5fl oz) whole milk

2 tbsp Greek yogurt or thick plain yogurt

150ml (5fl oz) double cream, whipped

250g (9oz) strawberries, thinly sliced

icing sugar, for dusting

1 Preheat the oven to 180°C (350°F/Gas 4) and line several baking sheets with baking parchment. Cream the butter and sugar until fluffy, then beat in the egg and vanilla. In a bowl, sift the flour, cocoa, and baking powder. Mix the dry ingredients and the milk into the batter alternately, a spoonful at a time. Fold in the yogurt.

2 Put 20 heaped tablespoons of the batter onto the baking sheets, spaced well apart. Dip a spoon in warm water and use the back to smooth their surfaces.

3 Bake for 12 minutes, until well risen. Cool for a few minutes, then turn onto a wire rack to cool.

4 Spread the cream onto half the cakes. Top with a layer of strawberries and a second cake. Dust with icing sugar and serve. These do not store and should be eaten on the day they are made.

Black and white whoopie pies

Fast becoming a modern classic, whoopie pies are a quick and easy way to please a crowd.

🥣 **40 MINS**

🍲 **12 MIN**

❄️ **FREEZABLE**

MAKES 10

175g (6oz) unsalted butter, softened

150g (5½ oz) soft light brown sugar

1 large egg, lightly beaten

1 tsp vanilla extract

225g (8oz) self-raising flour

75g (2½ oz) cocoa powder

1 tsp baking powder

150ml (5fl oz) whole milk

2 tbsp Greek yogurt or thick plain yogurt

FOR THE BUTTERCREAM

100g (3½ oz) unsalted butter, softened

200g (7oz) icing sugar

2 tsp vanilla extract

2 tsp milk, plus extra if needed

TO DECORATE

a little white and dark chocolate

200g (7oz) icing sugar

1 Preheat the oven to 180°C (350°F/Gas 4). Line several baking sheets with baking parchment. With a whisk, cream together the butter and brown sugar until light and fluffy, then beat in the egg and vanilla extract.

2 In a separate bowl, sift together the flour, cocoa, and baking powder. Gently fold the flour mixture and milk, alternately, into the egg mixture. Fold in the yogurt. Place 20 heaped tbsp of this mixture on the baking sheets. Leave space for it to spread out. Dip a spoon in warm water and use the back to smooth the pies.

3 Bake for around 12 minutes, until a skewer comes out clean. Cool on a wire rack.

4 Using a wooden spoon, mix together the buttercream ingredients, except the milk. Add the milk and beat for 5 minutes. Spread 1 tbsp onto the flat side of half of the cakes, and sandwich together with the other half.

5 With a vegetable peeler, make white and dark chocolate shavings. Put the icing sugar in a bowl and add enough water to make a thick icing. Spread the icing over the pies, and sprinkle with chocolate shavings.

Madeleines

Light and incredibly moreish, buttery madeleines make an elegant teatime treat.

🥣 15-20 MINS

🍲 10 MINS

❄️ FREEZABLE

SPECIAL EQUIPMENT

madeleine tin, or small 12-hole bun tin

electric hand-held whisk

MAKES 12

60g (2oz) unsalted butter, melted and cooled, plus extra for greasing

60g (2oz) self-raising flour, sifted, plus extra for dusting

60g (2oz) caster sugar

2 eggs, lightly beaten

1 tsp vanilla extract

icing sugar, for dusting

1 Preheat the oven to 180°C (350°F/Gas 4). Carefully brush a madeleine tin, or small 12-hole bun tin, with melted butter and dust with a little flour. Invert the tin, and tap to remove excess flour.

2 Put the sugar, eggs, and vanilla into a mixing bowl. Using an electric hand-held whisk, mix for 5 minutes until the mixture is pale, thick, and holds a trail (this is known as the "ribbon stage").

3 Sift the flour over the top and pour the melted butter down the side of the mixture. Using a large metal spoon, fold them in carefully and quickly, being careful not to knock out too much air.

4 Fill the hollows in the tins evenly with the batter and bake for 10 minutes. Remove from the oven and transfer to a wire rack to cool. Dust with icing sugar to serve.

Buttermilk scones

Home-made, these are one of the simplest and best teatime treats. Buttermilk makes the lightest scones.

🥣 15-20 MINS

🍲 12-15 MINS

SPECIAL EQUIPMENT

7cm (2¾ in) round pastry cutter

MAKES 6-8

60g (2oz) unsalted butter, chilled, and cut into pieces, plus extra for greasing

250g (9oz) strong white bread flour, plus extra for dusting

2 tsp baking powder

½ tsp salt

175ml (6fl oz) buttermilk, plus extra if needed

butter, jam, and clotted cream or thick double cream, to serve

1 Preheat the oven to 220°C (425°F/Gas 7). Line a baking sheet with baking parchment and grease it. Sift the flour, baking powder, and salt into a large chilled bowl. Put the butter in the bowl, keeping everything cold.

2 Rub with your fingertips until the mixture forms fine crumbs, working quickly. Make a well in the centre and, in a steady stream, pour in the buttermilk. Quickly toss with a fork. Do not over-mix.

3 Stir the mixture until the crumbs form a dough. Add a little more buttermilk if it seems dry. Turn onto a floured surface and knead for a few seconds; keep it rough, not smooth. Pat the dough out to a round 2cm (¾ in) thick.

4 Cut out with a 7cm (2¾ in) round pastry cutter. Pat out the trimmings and cut additional rounds until all the dough has been used. Arrange the scones so they are about 5cm (2in) apart on the prepared baking sheet. Bake in the hot oven for 12–15 minutes until lightly browned and risen. Scones should be eaten on the day they are baked, ideally warm from the oven. Spread with butter, jam, and clotted cream or thick double cream.

Biscuits and traybakes

Butter biscuits

These thin, elegant biscuits make a great anytime snack, especially with a glass of milk. They are decidedly moreish.

🥣 **15 MINS**

🍲 **10-15 MINS**

❄ **FREEZABLE**

SPECIAL EQUIPMENT

7cm (2¾ in) round cookie cutter

MAKES 30

1100g (3½ oz) caster sugar

225g (8oz) plain flour, sifted, plus extra for dusting

150g (5½ oz) unsalted butter, at room temperature and diced

1 egg yolk

1 tsp vanilla extract

1 Preheat the oven to 180°C (350°F/Gas 4). Keep several non-stick baking trays ready. Put the sugar, flour, and butter into a large bowl, or into the bowl of a food processor. Rub together, or pulse-blend, the ingredients until they look like fine breadcrumbs.

2 Add the egg yolk and vanilla extract, and bring the mixture together into a dough. Turn the dough out onto a lightly floured work surface and knead it briefly until smooth. Flour the dough and work surface well, and roll the dough out to a thickness of about 5mm (¼ in). Use a palette knife to move the dough around, to prevent sticking. If the dough is too sticky to roll well, chill for 15 minutes, then try again.

3 With the cookie cutter, cut out round biscuits and transfer them to the baking trays. Re-roll the pastry offcuts to 5mm (¼ in) thick. Cut out biscuits until all the dough is used. Bake in batches for 10–15 minutes until golden brown at the edges. Leave the biscuits to cool until firm enough to handle, then transfer to a wire rack.

Ginger biscuits

The little chunks of stem ginger bring warmth and spice to these biscuits. You can use a tablespoon of golden syrup or black treacle instead, if you prefer.

🥣 **20 MINS**

🍲 **24-30 MINS**

❄ **FREEZABLE**

MAKES 35

225g (8oz) butter, at room temperature

175g (6oz) light or dark soft brown sugar

1 tbsp syrup from a jar of stem ginger

1 large egg

350g (12oz) self-raising flour

1 heaped tbsp ground ginger

3 balls of stem ginger in syrup, drained and finely chopped

1 Preheat the oven to 190°C (375°F/Gas 5). Line two baking trays with parchment. In a bowl, mix the butter, sugar, and syrup together with an electric whisk until creamy. Mix in the egg until combined, then work in the flour, ground ginger, and stem ginger until the mixture comes together to form a soft dough.

2 Roll the dough into about 35 balls, each the size of a walnut, and place on the baking trays. Flatten them with your fingers, then bake in two batches for 12–15 minutes or until golden brown. Carefully transfer to a wire rack and leave to cool completely.

Viennese biscuits

These swirly Austrian biscuits are dipped in chocolate and look as good as they taste.

🥣 **10 MINS**

🍲 **15-20 MINS**

❄️ **FREEZABLE**

SPECIAL EQUIPMENT

piping bag and 2cm (¾ in) plain or star nozzler

MAKES 9

125g (4½ oz) unsalted butter, at room temperature, plus extra for greasing

60g (2oz) icing sugar

115g (4oz) gluten-free plain flour

30g (1oz) cornflour

2 tsp xanthan gum

¼ tsp gluten-free baking powder

½ tsp vanilla extract

115g (4oz) dark chocolate (at least 70 per cent cocoa solids), broken into even pieces

1 Preheat the oven to 190°C (375°F/Gas 5) and lightly grease 2 large baking trays. Place the butter and icing sugar in a large bowl and beat with an electric whisk until pale and fluffy.

2 Sift over the flours, xanthan, and baking powder. Add the vanilla extract, then beat again with the whisk until a soft dough forms.

3 Spoon the dough into a piping bag and, holding the nozzle with one hand while squeezing with the other, pipe 9 biscuits in a zigzag fashion onto the baking trays. Space them well apart as they will spread during baking.

4 Bake for 15–20 minutes or until pale golden brown. Leave to cool slightly before transferring to a wire rack to cool completely.

5 Place the chocolate in a heatproof bowl set over a pan of simmering water. Heat gently until the chocolate melts, stirring occasionally. Dip one-half of each biscuit in melted chocolate and leave to set on baking parchment.

Florentines

These crisp Italian biscuits are packed full of rich fruit and nuts
and coated with luxurious dark chocolate.

20 MINS

15-20 MINS

MAKES 16-20

60g (2oz) butter

60g (2oz) caster sugar

1 tbsp clear honey

60g (2oz) plain flour, sifted

45g (1½ oz) chopped mixed peel

45g (1½ oz) glacé cherries, finely
  chopped

45g (1½ oz) blanched almonds,
  finely chopped

1 tsp lemon juice

1 tbsp double cream

175g (6oz) good-quality dark
  chocolate, broken into pieces

1 Preheat the oven to 180°C
(350°F/Gas 4) and line 2 baking
trays with parchment.

2 Place the butter, sugar, and
honey into a small saucepan,
and melt gently over a low heat.
Allow it to cool until it is just
warm. Stir in all the other
ingredients except the chocolate.

3 Using a teaspoon, drop
spoonfuls of the mixture
onto the baking trays, leaving
space between them for the
biscuits to spread.

4 Bake for 10 minutes or until
golden, but do not let them
get too dark. Leave them on
the baking trays for 2–3 minutes,
before lifting them onto a wire rack
to cool completely.

5 Place the chocolate pieces
into a heatproof bowl set over
a pan of gently simmering water.

Make sure that the bowl is not
touching the water.

6 Once the chocolate has
melted, use a palette knife
to spread a thin layer of chocolate
on the bottom of each biscuit.
Place the biscuits chocolate-side
up on a wire rack to set. Spread a
second layer of chocolate over the
biscuits, then just before it sets,
make a wavy line in the chocolate
with a fork.

Rich chocolate biscuits

The key to baking these biscuits lies in good-quality cocoa powder and chocolate – it will make all the difference.

- 15 MINS
- 20 MINS
- ❄ FREEZABLE

MAKES 16

100g (3½ oz) butter, at room temperature

50g (1¾ oz) caster sugar

125g (4½ oz) plain flour

25g (scant 1oz) cocoa powder, melted

dark chocolate or milk chocolate, to decorate

1 Preheat the oven to 180°C (350°F/Gas 4). Line 2 baking trays with parchment. In a bowl, mix the butter and sugar together with an electric whisk or food mixer until pale and creamy. Sift in the flour and cocoa powder, and beat until the mixture comes together to form a dough. You may need to bring it together with your hands at the end.

2 Roll the dough into 16 walnut-sized balls and place them on the baking trays. Press the centre of each one with your thumb to flatten it, or use a fork, which will decorate it at the same time. Bake for 20 minutes, then transfer to a wire rack to cool completely. Drizzle over the melted chocolate, and allow to set before serving.

Raspberry sablés

Originating from Normandy, the name of these rich biscuits comes from the French word for "sand", as they have a light, crumbly texture.

🥣 **15 MINS, PLUS CHILLING**

🍲 **8-10 MINS**

❄ **FREEZABLE**

SPECIAL EQUIPMENT

7.5cm (3in) round cookie cutter

MAKES 12-16

150g (5½ oz) plain flour, plus extra for dusting

30g (1oz) ground almonds

85g (3oz) icing sugar

125g (4½ oz) butter, at room temperature

1 egg yolk

½ tsp almond extract

raspberry jam

1 Place all the ingredients, except the jam, in a food processor, and blend until the mixture forms a soft dough. If you do not have a food processor, beat the sugar, butter, and egg yolk together, then beat in the remaining ingredients (except for the jam) and knead to a soft dough. Wrap in cling film and chill for at least 30 minutes.

2 Preheat the oven to 190°C (375°F/Gas 5). Lightly grease 2 baking trays. Roll out the dough on a lightly floured work surface to a thickness of 3mm (⅛in), and cut out rounds with the biscuit cutter. Transfer to the baking trays. Re-roll the dough and cut out rounds until it has all been used. Do not overwork the dough or the biscuits will be tough.

3 Bake the biscuits for 8–10 minutes or until pale golden. Allow to cool slightly on the tray, then transfer to a wire rack to cool completely. To complete, sandwich 2 biscuits together with raspberry jam.

Gingerbread men

Making gingerbread men is quick and easy, and the decorating is definitely the most fun a child can have in the kitchen.

🥣 **20 MINS**

🍲 **10-12 MINS, PLUS COOLING**

❄ **FREEZABLE**

SPECIAL EQUIPMENT

11cm (4½ in) gingerbread man cutter

piping bag with thin nozzle (optional)

MAKES 16

4 tbsp golden syrup

300g (10oz) plain flour, plus extra for dusting

1 tsp bicarbonate of soda

1½ tsp ground ginger

1½ tsp mixed spice

100g (3½ oz) unsalted butter, softened and cut into cubes

150g (5½ oz) soft dark brown sugar

1 egg, lightly beaten

raisins, to decorate

icing sugar, sifted (optional)

1 Preheat the oven to 190°C (375°F/Gas 5). Heat the syrup to melt, then cool. Sift the flour, bicarbonate of soda, and spices into a bowl. Rub in the butter with your fingers until it looks like crumbs. Mix in the sugar.

2 Beat the egg into the syrup. Make a well in the flour mixture, pour in the syrup, and bring into a dough. On a floured work surface, knead it briefly until smooth. Flour the dough and roll it out to 5mm (¼in) thick.

3 Using an 11cm (4½ in) cutter, cut out as many shapes as possible. Transfer to non-stick baking sheets. Mix the offcuts of dough, re-roll, and cut out more shapes until all the dough is used.

4 Decorate the men with raisins, giving them eyes, a nose, and buttons down the front. Bake for 10–12 minutes until golden. Transfer carefully to a wire rack with a palette knife to cool completely.

5 If using, mix a little icing sugar in a bowl with enough water to form a thin icing. Transfer the icing into a piping bag with a thin nozzle; placing the bag into a jug to catch the drips first will help.

6 Decorate the men with the piped icing to resemble clothes, hair, or whatever you prefer; use your imagination (you can also use the icing to stick on other decorations). Leave to set completely before serving.

Pistachio and orange biscotti

These fragrant biscotti are delicious served either with coffee or dipped in a glass of sweet dessert wine.

🥣 **15 MINS**

🍲 **40-45 MINS**

❄ **FREEZABLE**

MAKES 25-30

100g (3½ oz) whole pistachios, shelled

225g (8oz) self-raising flour

100g (3½ oz) caster sugar

grated zest of 1 orange

2 eggs

1 tsp vanilla extract

50g (1¾ oz) unsalted butter, melted and cooled

1 Preheat the oven to 180°C (350°F/Gas 4). Spread the pistachios on an unlined baking sheet and bake in the oven for 5–10 minutes. Allow to cool, then rub in a clean tea towel to remove the skins and roughly chop.

2 Mix the flour, sugar, zest, and nuts together in a mixing bowl. In a separate bowl, whisk the eggs and vanilla extract with the butter. Then mix the wet and dry ingredients together to form a dough.

3 Turn the dough out onto a floured work surface and form into 2 logs, each 20cm (8in) x 7.5cm (3in). Place them on a baking sheet lined with silicone paper and bake for 20 minutes in the centre of the oven. Allow to cool slightly, then cut diagonally into 3–5cm (1¼–2in) thick slices with a serrated knife.

4 Return to the oven to bake for another 15 minutes, turning them after 10 minutes, until golden and hard to the touch. Then remove from the oven and allow to cool.

Almond macaroons

These almond meringue biscuits (not to be confused with French macarons) are crisp outside and chewy inside.

10 MINS

12-15 MINS

SPECIAL EQUIPMENT

sheets of edible wafer paper (optional)

MAKES 24

2 egg whites

225g (8oz) caster sugar

125g (4½ oz) ground almonds

30g (1oz) rice flour

a few drops of almond extract

24 blanched almonds

1 Preheat the oven to 180°C (350°F/Gas 4). Use an electric whisk to stiffen the egg whites. Gradually whisk in the sugar, a tablespoon at a time, to give a thick, glossy meringue. Fold in the ground almonds, rice flour, and almond extract until well combined.

2 Divide the wafer paper (if using) between 2 baking trays or line them with parchment. Use 2 teaspoons to scoop and shape the mixture, cleaning and drying the spoons between scoops. Place 4 teaspoons of the mixture in rounds, spaced apart, on each piece of edible wafer paper. Place a blanched almond in the centre of each biscuit.

3 Bake the macaroons in the centre of the oven for 12–15 minutes or until lightly golden. Transfer to a wire rack to cool completely, before tearing each biscuit from the paper. Macaroons are prone to sticking, but by using edible wafer paper it doesn't matter if the paper tears off with the biscuit.

Oat and raisin cookies

These crisp, crumbly cookies are packed full of fibre-filled oats and sweet raisins for a healthier treat.

🍲 10 MINS

🍲 15 MINS

❄ FREEZABLE

MAKES 15

150g (5½ oz) butter

100g (3½ oz) caster sugar

125g (4½ oz) self-raising flour, sifted

100g (3½ oz) oats

50g (1¾ oz) raisins

1 tsp bicarbonate of soda

1 Preheat the oven to 180°C (350°F/Gas 4). Melt the butter in a large saucepan over a gentle heat. Allow it to cool while you measure out the other ingredients.

2 Mix the sugar, flour, oats, and raisins into the cooled, melted butter and stir well.

3 In a cup, mix the bicarbonate of soda with 1 tbsp boiling water until it dissolves, then mix it well into the biscuit mixture.

4 Take 1 tbsp of the mixture and roll it into a ball between your hands. Flatten it slightly and put it on a baking tray. Repeat to use up all the dough, spacing them well apart on the tray, as they will spread.

5 Bake in the centre of the oven for 12–15 minutes until they turn golden brown. Remove the cookies from the oven and leave them to cool on their baking sheets for 5 minutes (they will break if you do not), then transfer them to a wire rack to cool completely.

Double chocolate chip cookies

The ultimate chocolate treat – try these freshly baked and still warm with a cold glass of milk.

🍲 10 MINS

🍲 15 MINS

❄ FREEZABLE

SPECIAL EQUIPMENT

electric hand-held whisk

MAKES 15

100g (3½ oz) butter, softened

100g (3½ oz) caster sugar

100g (3½ oz) soft light brown sugar

1 large egg, lightly beaten

1 tsp vanilla extract

150g (5½ oz) plain flour

25g (scant 1oz) cocoa powder

½ tsp baking powder

¼ tsp salt

1 tbsp whole milk

100g (3½ oz) chocolate chips

1 Preheat the oven to 180°C (350°F/Gas 4). In a large bowl, cream together the butter and sugars until light and fluffy, then beat in the egg and vanilla extract.

2 Sift the flour, cocoa powder, baking powder, and salt together, and mix it in to the cookie mixture, until it is well combined. Mix in the milk.

3 Fold in the chocolate chips. Place tablespoons of the biscuit mixture onto several baking sheets, spaced well apart as they will spread on cooking.

4 Bake the cookies in the centre of the oven for 15 minutes, until just cooked. Leave to cool on the baking sheets for 5 minutes before transferring them to a wire rack to cool completely.

HOW TO FREEZE

The baked cookies can be frozen in an airtight container for up to 6 months. Defrost thoroughly before eating.

Pistachio and cranberry oat cookies

Using pistachios and cranberries brings a healthy, chewy bite to these easy-to-make cookies.

🥣 **20 MINS**

🍲 **10-15 MINS**

❄️ **FREEZABLE**

SPECIAL EQUIPMENT

electric hand-held whisk

MAKES 24

100g (3½ oz) unsalted butter, softened

200g (7oz) soft light brown sugar

1 egg, lightly beaten

1 tsp vanilla extract

1 tbsp runny honey

125g (4½ oz) self-raising flour, sifted

125g (4½ oz) oats

pinch of salt

100g (3½ oz) pistachio nuts, lightly toasted and roughly chopped

100g (3½ oz) dried cranberries, roughly chopped

a little milk, if needed

1 Preheat the oven to 190°C (375°F/Gas 5). Put the butter and sugar in a bowl, and cream with an electric hand-held whisk until smooth. Add the egg, vanilla extract, and honey, and beat well.

2 Add the flour, oats, and salt, stirring with a wooden spoon to combine. Add the chopped nuts and cranberries, and mix until thoroughly combined. If the mixture is too stiff, add a little milk until it becomes pliable.

3 Take walnut-sized pieces and roll them into balls between your palms. Place on 2 or 3 baking sheets lined with parchment and flatten slightly, spacing them well apart on the tray.

4 Bake for 10–15 minutes until golden brown (you may need to do this in batches). Leave on the tray to cool, then transfer to a wire rack. These will keep in an airtight container for up to 5 days.

Carrot cake cookies

These soft cookies will become a real favourite; they have all the goodness of carrot cake in a bite-sized snack.

🥣 **15 MINS**

🍲 **12-15 MINS**

❄️ **FREEZABLE**

SPECIAL EQUIPMENT

electric hand-held whisk

MAKES 20

100g (3½ oz) butter, softened

100g (3½ oz) soft light brown sugar

100g (3½ oz) caster sugar

1 egg, lightly beaten

100g (3½ oz) plain flour

50g (1¾ oz) wholemeal flour

½ tsp baking powder

½ tsp ground cinnamon

100g (3½ oz) finely grated carrot

50g (1¾ oz) raisins

1 Preheat the oven to 180°C (350°F/Gas 4). In a large mixing bowl, cream together the butter and sugars with an electric hand- held whisk until light and fluffy. Add the egg and beat well to combine.

2 Sift the flours, baking powder, and cinnamon into the cookie mixture, tipping in any bran that is left in the sieve. Add the carrot and raisins and stir well.

3 Put heaped teaspoons of the cookie batter, spaced well apart, onto 2 baking trays lined with baking parchment.

4 Bake in the middle of the oven for 12–15 minutes, until golden brown and risen slightly.

5 Remove from the oven and cool for 5 minutes on the baking sheets before transferring to a wire rack to cool completely.

Peanut butter cookies

These sweet, salty cookies are perfect for anyone who loves peanut butter... and biscuits!

🥣 **10 MINS**

🍲 **10-12 MINS**

❄️ **FREEZABLE**

SPECIAL EQUIPMENT

electric hand-held whisk

MAKES 20-24

200g (7oz) butter, softened

150g (5½ oz) soft light brown sugar

2 eggs, lightly beaten

1 tsp vanilla extract

200g (7oz) crunchy peanut butter

300g (10oz) plain flour, sifted

½ tsp salt

1 Preheat the oven to 180°C (350°F/Gas 4). Put the butter and sugar in a bowl and cream together with an electric hand-held whisk until fluffy. Add the eggs and vanilla, and whisk well. Whisk in the peanut butter, then fold in the flour and salt just until the mixture is well combined.

2 Place tablespoonfuls of the mixture onto non-stick baking sheets, spaced apart, and press down with the back of a fork in a criss-cross pattern. Dip the fork in water between each cookie, to stop it sticking. This decorates the biscuits and helps them to spread when cooking. Bake for 10–12 minutes, until lightly coloured.

3 Remove from the oven, and cool for 5 minutes on the baking sheets before transferring to a wire rack to cool completely.

HOW TO FREEZE

The baked cookies can be frozen in an airtight container. Defrost thoroughly and eat within 12 weeks.

Slice and bake butter biscuits

These biscuits are so convenient, as the dough can be stored uncooked in the fridge or freezer to bake when needed.

⊟ 20 MINS

⊟ 10-12 MINS

❄ FREEZABLE

SPECIAL EQUIPMENT

electric hand-held whisk

MAKES 20

200g (7oz) butter, softened

100g (3½oz) caster sugar, plus extra for dusting

1 tsp vanilla extract

300g (10oz) plain flour, sifted

1 Put the butter and sugar in a large bowl and cream them with an electric hand-held whisk until light and fluffy. Beat in the vanilla. Mix in the flour to form a stiff dough.

2 Divide the mixture into 2, and roll each piece out to make a fat log about 6cm (2½ in) in diameter and 20cm (8in) long.

Sprinkle a work surface with caster sugar, and roll the biscuit log in it, to coat the outside in sugar.

3 Wrap the dough logs in cling film and refrigerate for at least 2 hours, and up to 3 days.

4 When ready to bake, preheat the oven to 180°C (350°F/ Gas 4). Cut off as much of the log as you need, then slice the hardened dough into 1cm- (½ in-) thick disks.

5 Place on a lined baking sheet and bake for 10–12 minutes, until golden brown at the edges. Leave to cool for 5 minutes before transferring to a wire rack to cool.

HOW TO FREEZE

This dough can be frozen for up to 12 weeks. Cut off what you need with a serrated knife, defrost for 30 minutes, then slice and bake as usual.

Chocolate and hazelnut brownies

A classic American recipe, these brownies are moist and squidgy in the centre, and filled with toasted nuts.

 25 MINS

12-15 MINS

SPECIAL EQUIPMENT

23 x 30cm (9 x 12in) brownie tin, or similar

MAKES 24

175g (6oz) unsalted butter, cut into cubes

300g (10oz) good-quality dark chocolate, broken into pieces

300g (10oz) caster sugar

4 large eggs, lightly beaten

200g (7oz) plain flour, sifted

25g (scant 1oz) cocoa powder, sifted, plus extra for dusting

100g (3½ oz) hazelnuts, toasted and chopped

1 Preheat the oven to 200°C (400°F/Gas 6). Line the base and sides of a 23 x 30cm (9 x 12in) brownie tin, or similar, with baking parchment. Some should hang over the sides. Place the butter and chocolate in a heatproof bowl over a pan of simmering water. The bowl should not touch the water.

2 Melt the butter and chocolate, stirring until smooth. Remove and leave to cool. Once the mixture has cooled, mix in the sugar. Now add the eggs, a little at a time, mixing well between additions.

3 Fold in the flour and cocoa until the batter is smooth. Stir in the nuts to distribute them evenly; the batter should be thick.

4 Pour into the prepared tin and spread so the mixture fills the corners. Smooth the top. Bake for 12–15 minutes, or until just firm to the touch but still soft underneath. A skewer inserted should come out coated with a little batter. Remove from the oven.

5 Leave the brownie to cool completely in the tin to maintain the soft centre. Lift the brownie from the tin using the edges of the parchment to get a good grip. Using a long, sharp, or serrated knife, score the surface of the brownie into 24 even pieces.

6 Cut the brownie into 24 pieces, dipping the knife in hot water between cuts and wiping it dry. Sift cocoa powder over the brownies. These will store in an airtight container for up to 3 days.

Sour cherry and chocolate brownies

The sharp flavour and chewy texture of the cherries contrast wonderfully with the rich, dark chocolate.

 15 MINS

20-25 MINS

 FREEZABLE

SPECIAL EQUIPMENT

23 x 30cm (9 x 12in) brownie tin, or similar

MAKES 16

150g (5½ oz) unsalted butter, cut into cubes

150g (5½ oz) good-quality dark chocolate, broken into pieces

250g (9oz) soft light brown muscovado sugar

3 eggs, lightly beaten

1 tsp vanilla extract

150g (5½ oz) self-raising flour, sifted

100g (3½ oz) dried sour cherries

100g (3½ oz) dark chocolate chunks

1 Preheat the oven to 180°C (350°F/Gas 4). Line a 23 x 30cm (9 x 12in) brownie tin, or similar, with baking parchment. Melt the butter and chocolate in a heatproof bowl over simmering water (the bowl should not touch the water). Stir in the sugar, and cool slightly.

2 Mix the eggs and vanilla extract into the chocolate mixture. Pour the wet mix into the sifted flour and fold together, being careful not to over-mix. Fold in the sour cherries and chocolate chunks.

3 Pour the brownie mixture into the tin and bake in the centre of the oven for 20–25 minutes. It is ready when the edges are firm, but the middle is soft to the touch.

4 Leave the brownie to cool in the tin for 5 minutes. Turn out and cut into 16 squares. Put the brownies onto a wire rack to cool. These will store in an airtight container for up to 3 days.

Sticky date flapjacks

Healthy, baked oat squares such as these make a great lunchbox addition. You can also choose to remove the dates and make plain, crispy flapjacks instead.

25 MINS

45 MINS

SPECIAL EQUIPMENT

20cm (8in) square tin

MAKES 16 SQUARES

200g (7oz) stoned dates (medjool are best), chopped

½ tsp bicarbonate of soda

200g (7oz) butter

200g (7oz) light soft brown sugar

2 tbsp golden syrup

300g (10oz) rolled oats

1 Preheat the oven to 160°C (325°F/Gas 3). Line the tin with baking parchment. Place the dates and bicarbonate of soda in a pan with enough water to cover, simmer for 5 minutes, then drain, reserving the liquid. Whizz to a purée in a blender with 3 tablespoons of the liquid, then set aside.

2 Melt the butter, sugar, and syrup together in a large pan, stirring until the mixture forms a smooth sauce (you might need to give it a quick whisk to bring it together). Stir in the oats, then press half the mixture into the base of the tin.

3 Spread the date purée over the top of the oats, then spoon the remaining oat mixture over the top, gently easing it over the dates. Bake for 40 minutes or until golden brown. Leave to cool in the tin for 10 minutes, then cut into 16 squares. Leave to cool completely in the tin before serving.bake as usual.

Toffee apple traybake

Rich sauce and fresh apples make this heartwarming cake a firm autumn favourite. If short on time, use a ready-made toffee sauce.

20 MINS

45 MINS

SPECIAL EQUIPMENT

22 x 30cm (8¾ x 12in) tin

MAKES 18 SQUARES

350g (12oz) Bramley apples, peeled, cored, and thinly sliced

squeeze of lemon juice

350g (12oz) self-raising flour

2 tsp baking powder

350g (12oz) light soft brown sugar

4 large eggs, lightly beaten

225g (8oz) butter, melted

1 tbsp caster sugar

FOR THE TOFFEE SAUCE

100g (3½ oz) butter

100g (3½ oz) light soft brown sugar

1 tbsp lemon juice

salt

1 Preheat the oven to 180°C (350°F/Gas 4). Line the base and sides of the tin with baking parchment. Place the apple slices in a bowl and toss with the lemon juice to stop them from turning brown while you make the cake mixture.

2 Sift the flour into a large mixing bowl, add the baking powder and brown sugar, and stir well. Mix in the eggs and the butter to make a smooth batter. Pour into the tin and smooth the top. Arrange the apple slices in 3 or 4 long lines along the top of the mixture and sprinkle with the caster sugar. Bake for 45 minutes or until the cake is firm to the touch and a skewer inserted into the centre comes out clean.

3 Meanwhile, make the sauce by melting the butter, sugar, and lemon juice in a pan with a pinch of salt, whisking with an electric whisk until the mixture is thick, melted, and smooth. Leave to cool slightly. Pour the sauce over the cake while it is still in the tin, gently brushing the sauce all over the top of the cake. Serve warm or cold cut into squares.

Spiced carrot and orange cake

Grated carrots really help keep this cake moist and add flavour, too. But it's the mixed spice that makes this cake just a little bit different from standard carrot cake recipes.

🥣 20 MINS

🍲 30 MINS

❄ FREEZABLE

SPECIAL EQUIPMENT

20cm (8in) square cake tin

electric hand whisk

MAKES 16

175g (6oz) self-raising flour

1 tsp ground cinnamon

1 tsp mixed spice

½ tsp bicarbonate of soda

100g (3½ oz) light soft brown sugar or dark soft brown sugar

150ml (5fl oz) sunflower oil or light olive oil

2 large eggs

75g (2½ oz) golden syrup

125g (4½ oz) carrots, coarsely grated

zest of 1 orange

FOR THE ICING

75g (2½ oz) icing sugar

100g (3½ oz) cream cheese, at room temperature

1–2 tbsp orange juice

zest of 1 orange, plus extra to decorate (optional)

1 Preheat the oven to 180°C (350°F/Gas 4). Line the base and sides of a cake tin with baking parchment. In a large bowl, mix together the flour, spices, bicarbonate of soda, and sugar. In another bowl, mix the oil, eggs, and syrup together, then combine with the dry ingredients. Stir in the carrots and orange zest, transfer to the tin, and level the top. Bake for 30 minutes, or until firm to the touch. Leave to cool in the tin for 5 minutes, then cool completely on a wire rack.

2 For the icing, sift the icing sugar into a bowl, add the cream cheese, orange juice, and orange zest, and whisk with an electric hand whisk until the mixture becomes thick. When the cake is cool, spread the icing over the top. Decorate with extra orange zest, if using, and cut into 16 squares, to serve.

Hummingbird slice

The bananas and crushed pineapple in this cake make it extremely moist and help it to last for days.

🥣 20 MINS

🍲 45-50 MINS

SPECIAL EQUIPMENT

23cm (9in) square cake tin

electric hand-held whisk

MAKES 25 SQUARES

butter, for greasing

75g (2½ oz) plain flour

150g (5½ oz) self-raising flour

½ tsp bicarbonate of soda

1 tsp ground cinnamon

180g (6¼ oz) soft light brown sugar

120ml (4fl oz) sunflower oil

3 eggs, lightly beaten

3 bananas, approx. 320g (11oz) in total, mashed

440g can crushed pineapple, drained

FOR THE TOPPING

40g (1¼ oz) unsalted butter, softened

85g (3oz) full-fat cream cheese

150g (5½ oz) icing sugar

1 Preheat the oven to 180°C (350°F/Gas 4). Grease a 23cm (9in) square cake tin and line the base with baking parchment.

2 Sift the flours, bicarbonate of soda, and cinnamon into a large bowl. Stir in the sugar.

3 Place the oil and eggs in a jug and whisk well. Pour into the dry ingredients. Stir in the bananas and pineapple. Transfer to the tin. Bake for 45–50 minutes, or until a skewer comes out clean.

4 Meanwhile, prepare the topping. Place the butter and cream cheese in a bowl and whisk together using an electric hand-held whisk. Sift the icing sugar and whisk it into the mixture.

5 Leave the cake in the tin for 10 minutes, then turn onto a wire rack and cool completely. Place on a serving plate, spread with the icing, and cut into squares to serve.

Shortbread

This is the classic Scottish shortbread, which should be pale in colour
and crumbly with a light buttery flavour.

 15 MINS, PLUS CHILLING

30–40 MINS

SPECIAL EQUIPMENT

18cm (7in) loose-bottomed round
cake tin

electric hand-held whisk

MAKES 8 WEDGES

150g (5½ oz) unsalted butter,
softened, plus extra for greasing

75g (2½ oz) caster sugar, plus extra
for sprinkling

175g (6oz) plain flour

50g (1¾ oz) cornflour

1 Preheat the oven to 160°C
(325°F/Gas 3). Grease an 18cm
(7in) loose-bottomed round cake
tin and line with parchment. Place
the softened butter and sugar in
a large bowl. Cream together with
an electric hand-held whisk until
light and fluffy.

2 Stir in the flour and cornflour
very gently, stopping as soon
as the flours are mixed in. Bring
together with your hands to form
a very rough, crumbly dough.
Transfer to the cake tin and firmly
push the dough down with your
hands to form a compact and
even layer.

3 With a sharp knife, lightly
score the shortbread into 8
wedges. Prick it all over with a
fork to make a decorative pattern.
Cover with cling film and chill
for 1 hour.

4 Bake in the centre of the oven
for 30–40 minutes. Cover with
foil if it browns quickly. Take it out
of the oven and re-score the
wedges with a sharp knife. While
it is still warm, sprinkle a thin layer
of caster sugar evenly over the top.
When completely cool, turn it
gently out of its tin and break or
cut it into wedges along the scored
lines. This shortbread keeps in an
airtight container for up to 5 days.

Apricot crumble shortbread

This variation on classic shortbread has a buttery crumb topping and a chunky, lemony apricot layer beneath – a delicious, fruit-filled teatime treat.

🥣 **20 MINS PLUS CHILLING**

🍲 **1 HR 15 MINS**

SPECIAL EQUIPMENT

12.5 x 35.5cm (5¼ x 14¼ in) baking tin

electric hand whisk or mixer

MAKES 10 BARS OR 20 SQUARES

200g (7oz) butter, softened

100g (3½ oz) caster sugar

200g (7oz) plain flour

100g (3½ oz) cornflour

250g (9oz) apricots, skinned, stoned and roughly chopped

grated zest of ½ lemon

FOR THE CRUMBLE TOPPING

75g (2½ oz) butter, diced

150g (5½ oz) plain flour

75g (2½ oz) demerara sugar or caster sugar

1 Line the baking tin with baking parchment. Cream the butter and sugar together in a bowl with an electric hand whisk or mixer until pale and creamy. Sift in the flour and cornflour and combine well so that the mix comes together to form a dough. (You'll probably need to use your hands to bring it together at the end.) Knead the dough lightly until smooth, then push it evenly into the base of the tin and smooth the top. Chill in the fridge for at least 1 hour, or until firm.

2 Preheat the oven to 180°C (350°F/Gas 4). To make the crumble topping, put the butter and flour into a mixing bowl. Rub the butter into the flour with your fingertips until the mixture resembles breadcrumbs. Add the sugar and stir it in. Scatter the apricots and lemon zest evenly over the chilled shortbread base, then top with the crumble mixture, pressing it down quite firmly.

3 Bake for 1¼ hours, or until a skewer inserted into the centre comes out clean with no uncooked mixture on it (it might be a bit damp from the fruit, though). Leave to cool in the tin. When cold, remove from the tin and divide into either 10 bars or 20 squares.

Chocolate strawberry shortcakes

These delightful little cakes are perfect served with afternoon tea. For a party canapé, cut smaller versions, sandwich with a single slice of strawberry, and serve to your guests.

 15 MINS

🍲 **10 MINS**

SPECIAL EQUIPMENT

7.5cm (3in) round cutter

SERVES 6

200g (7oz) plain flour

30g (1oz) cocoa powder

2 tsp baking powder

60g (2oz) butter, softened

60g (2oz) caster sugar, plus extra for sweetening

1 large egg

1 tsp vanilla extract

6 tbsp milk

225g (8oz) strawberries

150ml (5fl oz) double cream, whipped

1 Preheat the oven to 230°C (450°F/Gas 8). Sift the flour, cocoa, and baking powder into a bowl. Add the butter and rub in with fingertips. Stir in the sugar. Beat the egg with the vanilla and stir in. Add enough milk to form a soft, but not sticky, dough. Knead gently until smooth.

2 Pat out the dough to about 1cm (½ in) thick. Cut into 6 rounds using a 7.5cm (3in) cutter. Place on a lightly greased baking sheet. Bake in the oven for about 10 minutes until risen and the bases sound hollow when tapped. Transfer to a wire rack to cool for 5–10 minutes.

3 Halve 3 strawberries for decoration, leaving the calyces intact, and reserve. Hull and slice the remaining strawberries in half, and sweeten with a little caster sugar, if necessary.

4 Split the shortcakes and sandwich with the sliced strawberries and some of the cream. Top with the remaining cream and decorate with the reserved, halved strawberries.

Marbled millionaire's shortbread

A modern classic, this is extremely sweet and rich, just as it should be.

🥣 **45 MINS**

🍲 **30-45 MINS**

❄️ **FREEZABLE**

SPECIAL EQUIPMENT

20cm (8in) square cake tin

MAKES 16 SQUARES

FOR THE SHORTBREAD

175g (6oz) unsalted butter, softened, plus extra for greasing

200g (7oz) plain flour

100g (3½ oz) caster sugar

FOR THE CARAMEL FILLING

50g (1¾ oz) unsalted butter

50g (1¾ oz) light brown sugar

400g can of condensed milk

FOR THE CHOCOLATE TOPPING

200g (7oz) milk chocolate

25g (scant 1oz) unsalted butter

50g (1¾ oz) dark chocolate

1 Preheat the oven to 160°C (325°F/Gas 3). Grease a 20cm (8in) square cake tin and line with baking parchment. For the shortbread, put the flour, butter, and sugar in a bowl and rub together to make crumbs. Press into the tin. Bake for 35–40 minutes until golden brown. Leave to cool.

2 For the caramel, melt the butter and sugar in a heavy-based saucepan over a medium heat. Add the condensed milk and bring to the boil, stirring. Reduce the heat and stir for 5 minutes until it thickens and is a light caramel colour. Pour over the shortbread and leave to cool.

3 To make the topping, place the milk chocolate and butter in a heatproof bowl over simmering water, until just melted. Melt the dark chocolate in another bowl.

4 Spread the milk chocolate over the caramel. Pour the dark chocolate over in a zigzag and drag a skewer through for a marbled effect. Leave to cool before cutting into 16 squares. These keep in an airtight container for up to 5 days.

Pecan sandies

These addictive cookies are so-called because they have the texture (though not the taste!) of fine sand.

🥣 **15 MINS, PLUS CHILLING**

🍲 **15 MIN**

❄️ **FREEZABLE**

SPECIAL EQUIPMENT

electric hand-held whisk

MAKES 18-20

100g (3½ oz) unsalted butter, softened

50g (1¾ oz) soft, light brown sugar

50g (1¾ oz) caster sugar

½ tsp vanilla extract

1 egg yolk

150g (5½ oz) plain flour, sifted, plus extra for dusting

75g (2½ oz) pecan nuts, chopped

1 Preheat the oven to 180°C (350°F/Gas 4). In a large bowl, cream together the butter and sugars with an electric hand-held whisk, until light and fluffy. Add the vanilla extract and the egg yolk, and mix well to combine. Fold in the flour and then the pecans. Bring it together to form a rough dough.

2 Turn the dough out onto a lightly floured work surface and knead it to form a smooth dough. Roll into a log about 20cm (8in) long. If the dough seems too soft to cut, chill it for 30 minutes to allow it to firm up.

3 Slice 1cm (½ in) disks from the log, and place them a little apart on 2 baking sheets lined with baking parchment. Bake in the top of the oven for 15 minutes, until golden at the edges. Leave on the sheets for a few minutes, then transfer to a wire rack to cool.

HOW TO FREEZE

There's nothing better than the aroma and flavour of just-baked biscuits. At the end of step 2, freeze the dough for up to 12 weeks. Now you can have fresh-baked biscuits at any time.

Raspberry towers

This easy yet impressive dessert is perfect for entertaining and can be assembled at the last minute.

⏱ 30 MINS, PLUS CHILLING

🍲 35MINS

❄ FREEZABLE

SPECIAL EQUIPMENT

7cm (2¾ in) round cookie cutter

SERVES 4

75g (2½oz) butter

125g (4½oz) caster sugar

1 egg yolk

½ tsp vanilla extract

pinch of salt

150g (5½oz) plain flour, sifted, plus extra for dusting

200ml (7fl oz) double cream

1 tbsp icing sugar, plus extra for dusting

300g (10oz) raspberries

1 Beat the butter and caster sugar together until fluffy. Beat in the yolk, vanilla, and salt. Stir in the flour to make a dough. Wrap in cling film and chill for 30 minutes. Preheat the oven to 180°C (350°F/Gas 4).

2 Roll out the dough as thinly as possible on a floured surface and cut out 12 rounds with a 7cm (2¾ in) cookie cutter. Any leftover dough can be frozen.

3 Bake for 10 minutes on a baking tray lined with baking parchment, until golden at the edges. Leave on the tray for a couple of minutes, then transfer to a wire rack to cool completely.

4 Whip the cream with the icing sugar until stiff. Spread a spoonful of cream on a biscuit and cover with raspberries. Take a second biscuit and spread a thin layer of cream underneath. Stick it on top. Repeat, finishing the tower with the nicest-looking biscuit. Dust with icing sugar to serve.

White chocolate macadamia blondies

A white chocolate version of the ever-popular brownie, studded with indulgent macadamia nuts.

⏱ 15 MINS

🍲 20 MINS

❄ FREEZABLE

SPECIAL EQUIPMENT

23 x 30cm (9 x 12in) brownie tin, or similar

MAKES 24

300g (10oz) white chocolate, broken into pieces

175g (6oz) unsalted butter, cut into cubes

300g (10oz) caster sugar

4 large eggs, lightly beaten

225g (8oz) plain flour

100g (3½oz) macadamia nuts, roughly chopped

1 Preheat the oven to 200°C (400°F/Gas 6). Line the base and sides of a 23 x 30cm (9 x 12in) brownie tin, or similar, with baking parchment. In a heatproof bowl set over simmering water, melt the chocolate and butter. Do not let the bowl touch the water. Remove and let cool for 20 minutes.

2 Once the chocolate has melted, mix in the sugar (the mixture may become thick and grainy, but the eggs will loosen it). Using a balloon whisk, beat in the eggs a little at a time, making sure each is well mixed in before you add the next. Sift in the flour, gently fold it in, then stir in the nuts.

3 Pour the mixture into the tin and gently spread it out into the corners. Bake for 20 minutes or until just firm to the touch on top, but still soft underneath. Leave to cool completely in the tin, then cut into 24 squares, or fewer rectangles for bigger blondies.

HOW TO STORE

The blondies will keep in an airtight container for 5 days, and will become more moist and dense in texture.

Baklava

This crispy Middle Eastern confection, filled with chopped nuts and spices and drenched in honey syrup, has long been a favourite.

  50-55 MINS

1 HR 15 MINS-1 HR 30 MINS

SPECIAL EQUIPMENT

30 x 40cm (12 x 16in) baking tray with deep sides

sugar thermometer (optional)

MAKES 36

250g (9oz) shelled unsalted pistachio nuts, coarsely chopped

250g (9oz) walnut pieces, coarsely chopped

250g (9oz) caster sugar

2 tsp ground cinnamon

large pinch of ground cloves

500g pack of filo pastry

250g (9oz) unsalted butter, plus extra for greasing

250ml (9fl oz) honey

juice of 1 lemon

3 tbsp orange flower water

1 Set aside 3–4 tablespoons of the chopped pistachios for decoration. Place the remainder in a bowl with the walnuts, 50g (1¾ oz) of the sugar, cinnamon, and cloves. Stir to mix.

2 Preheat the oven to 180°C (350°F/Gas 4). Lay a damp, clean tea towel on a work surface, unroll the filo sheets on it, and cover with a second dampened towel. Melt the butter in a small saucepan. Brush the baking tin with a little butter. Take a sheet of filo and line the tin with it, folding over one end to fit.

3 Brush the filo with butter, and gently press it into the corners and sides of the tin. Lay another sheet on top, brush it with butter, and press it into the tin as before. Continue layering the filo, buttering each sheet, until one-third has been used.

Scatter half the nut filling over the top sheet.

4 Layer another third of the filo sheets as before, then sprinkle the remaining nut filling over it. Layer the remaining sheets in the same manner. Trim off the excess with a knife. Brush with butter, and pour any remaining butter on top. With a small knife, cut diagonal lines, 1cm (½ in) deep, in the filo to mark out 4cm (1½ in) diamond shapes. Do not press down when cutting. Bake on the low shelf of the oven for 1¼–1½ hours until golden. A skewer inserted in the centre for 30 seconds should come out clean.

5 For the syrup, place the remaining sugar and 250ml (9fl oz) water in a pan, and heat until dissolved, stirring occasionally. Pour in the honey and stir to mix. Boil for about 25

minutes, without stirring, until the syrup reaches the soft ball stage, 115°C (239°F) on the sugar thermometer. To test without a thermometer, take the pan off the heat and dip a teaspoon in the hot syrup. Let the syrup cool for 2–3 seconds, then take a little between your finger and thumb; a soft ball should form. Remove the syrup from the heat and let it cool to lukewarm. Add the lemon juice and orange flower water. Remove the tin from the oven and immediately pour the syrup over the pastries. With a sharp knife, cut along the marked lines, almost to the bottom, then let the pastries cool.

6 Cut through the marked lines completely. Carefully lift out the pastries with a palette knife and arrange them on a dessert plate. Sprinkle the top of each pastry with the reserved chopped pistachio nuts.

Parmesan and rosemary thins

These biscuits are light and elegant, and are equally good served as an appetizer or after dinner with cheese.

🥣 **10 MINS, PLUS CHILLING**

🍲 **15 MINS, PLUS COOLING**

❄️ **FREEZABLE**

SPECIAL EQUIPMENT

food processor (optional)

6cm (2½ in) round cutter

SERVES 15–20

60g (2oz) unsalted butter, softened and cut into cubes

75g (2½ oz) plain flour, plus extra for dusting

60g (2oz) finely grated Parmesan cheese

freshly ground black pepper

1 tbsp chopped rosemary, thyme, or basil leaves

1 Place the butter and flour in a bowl, or a food processor. Rub with your fingertips, or pulse-blend, until the mixture resembles crumbs. Mix in the Parmesan, pepper, and herbs. Bring together to a dough.

2 Turn out onto a floured surface and briefly knead. Wrap in cling film and chill for 1 hour.

3 Preheat the oven to 180°C (350°F/Gas 4). Turn out the dough onto a floured surface.

4 Roll the dough out to 2mm (¹⁄₁₂ in) thick and cut out biscuits with a 6cm (2½ in) round cutter. Place on non-stick baking sheets and bake for 10 minutes. Turn and bake for a further 5 minutes.

5 Remove from the oven and leave on the trays for 5 minutes before transferring to a wire rack to cool completely. These keep in an airtight container for up to 3 days.

HOW TO FREEZE

Open-freeze the unbaked biscuits, then transfer to a large freezer bag for up to 12 weeks.

Multi-seed crackers

These can be adapted using a mixture of the seeds you like. Be sure to use the larger seeds for decorating.

🥣 **20 MINS**

🍲 **12-15 MINS**

SPECIAL EQUIPMENT

food processor (optional)

MAKES 45–50

150g (5½ oz) wholemeal flour

75g (2½ oz) plain flour, plus extra for dusting

50g (1¾ oz) butter, in pieces, softened

½ tsp fine salt

2 tbsp sesame seeds

2 tbsp linseeds

2 tbsp pumpkin seeds, plus extra for decorating

2 tbsp sunflower seeds, plus extra for decorating

1 tbsp clear honey

1 egg white

1 Preheat the oven to 200°C (400°F/Gas 6). In a large bowl with your fingertips, or in a food processor using the pulse-blend setting, blend the flours, butter, and salt until the mixture resembles fine crumbs. Mix in all the seeds.

2 Dissolve the honey in 100ml (3½ fl oz) of warm water. Make a well in the flour and mix in the water to form a soft dough.

3 Turn the dough onto a floured surface and knead it briefly. Roll out as thinly as possible – aim for 1–2mm (¹⁄₂₄–¹⁄₁₂ in) thick.

4 Cut the dough into 4 x 6cm (1½ x 2½ in) crackers. Leave on the work surface.

5 Whisk the egg white with ½ tbsp of water and brush the crackers. Scatter the additional pumpkin and sunflower seeds over, and gently press in.

6 Transfer to 2 baking sheets using a fish slice, and bake for 12–15 minutes, turning carefully halfway, or until both sides are crisp and golden brown. Leave to cool on their trays. Store in an airtight container for up to 2 weeks.

Tarts and pies

Lamb and potato pie

For some great comfort food on cool spring evenings, this is a great way to use up leftover roast lamb.

 20 MINS

50 MINS

SPECIAL EQUIPMENT

18cm (7in) round pie dish

SERVES 4

450g (1lb) potatoes, peeled and quartered

1 tbsp olive oil

1 onion, finely chopped

1 leek, trimmed and sliced

4 baby turnips, peeled and quartered

handful of rosemary sprigs, leaves picked and chopped

200g (7oz) leftover roast lamb, roughly shredded or sliced

salt and freshly ground black pepper

1 tbsp plain flour

300ml (10fl oz) hot vegetable stock

2-3 tsp mint sauce

250g (9oz) shortcrust pastry

1 egg, lightly beaten, for egg wash

1 Preheat the oven to 200°C (400°F/Gas 6). Cook the potatoes in a pan of boiling salted water for about 15 minutes until soft; drain and set aside. Heat the oil in a large pan over a low heat. Add the onion, leek, and turnips, and sweat gently for about 5 minutes until soft and translucent. Stir through the rosemary and add the lamb. Season with salt and pepper.

2 Tip in the flour and stir through, then pour in the stock. Keep stirring for about 10 minutes until the liquid begins to thicken, then add the reserved potatoes and stir in the mint sauce. Simmer for a further 10 minutes. Allow to cool slightly.

3 Divide the pastry into 2 pieces, one a little larger than the other. Roll out the larger piece into a large circle on a floured work surface. Use to line the pie dish, letting the pastry hang over the edges. Roll out the other piece to make the lid for the top of the pie.

4 Spoon the lamb mixture into the pastry shell, then sit the pastry lid on top. Pinch together the edges of the pastry to seal. Trim away the excess. Brush with a little egg wash and bake for 40–50 minutes until the pastry is golden. Leave to cool in the dish for at least 15 minutes before serving. Cut into slices and serve.

Chicken and pea filo pie

This impressive-looking pie of baby new potatoes, peas, and chicken is actually simple and quick to make. Use leftover roast chicken pieces instead of fresh if they need eating up.

20 MINS

30 MINS

❄ FREEZABLE

SPECIAL EQUIPMENT

18cm (7in) square pie or cake tin

SERVES 6

350g (12oz) skinless chicken breasts

250g (9oz) baby new potatoes, quartered

200ml (7fl oz) chicken stock

125g (4½ oz) peas (shelled weight)

12 sheets filo pastry

50g (1¾ oz) butter, melted, plus extra if needed

1-2 tbsp mild curry powder

salt and freshly ground black pepper

1 Cook the chicken and the potatoes in the stock in a medium-sized saucepan for about 10 minutes, or until both are tender, adding the peas for the last 5 minutes of cooking time. Drain, reserving the stock. Leave to cool, then cut the chicken into neat pieces.

2 Preheat the oven to 200°C (400°F/Gas 6). Lightly brush 6 sheets of the filo pastry with the melted butter. Use them to line the bottom of the pie or cake tin, allowing them to overlap the sides.

3 Put the chicken, potatoes, peas, and curry powder in a mixing bowl. Moisten with 3–4 tbsp of the reserved chicken stock, using just enough to wet the mixture and produce a little gravy, but without adding so much that it soaks the pastry. Toss the ingredients together and season well with salt and pepper.

4 Spoon the chicken filling into the filo pastry shell. Fold the pastry edges in towards the middle, and top the pie with the remaining 6 filo sheets, each brushed with a little melted butter. Tuck the edges of the pastry down neatly at the sides, and make sure that the top is well glazed with melted butter. Bake in the oven for 20–30 minutes until the pastry is cooked and golden. Serve hot.

Mini chicken, leek, and mushroom pies

Small in size but big in taste, these delicious morsels contain a creamy filling of winter produce flavoured with garlic and wine. Choose a small leek for a sweeter flavour.

🥣 15 MINS

🍲 50 MINS

❄ FREEZABLE

SPECIAL EQUIPMENT

6cm (2½ in) and 5cm (2in) biscuit cutters

12-hole mini muffin tin

MAKES 12

1 tbsp olive oil

25g (scant 1oz) butter

1 small carrot, finely chopped

1 small celery stick, finely chopped

1 small leek, white part only, trimmed and finely chopped

1 small garlic clove, grated or finely chopped

100g (3½ oz) chestnut mushrooms, diced

250g (9oz) skinless chicken breasts, diced

1 tbsp chopped thyme leaves

grated zest of ½ lemon

3 tbsp dry white wine

120ml (4fl oz) double cream

salt and freshly ground black pepper

1½ sheets ready-rolled puff pastry

1 egg, lightly beaten, for egg wash

mixed green leaves and herbs, to serve

1 Heat the oil and butter in a frying pan over a low heat. Add the carrot and celery, and gently sweat for about 5 minutes until soft. Add the leek and sweat for a few minutes until softened. Stir in the garlic and cook for 30 seconds, before adding the mushrooms. Cook, stirring occasionally, for a further 5 minutes.

2 Increase the heat slightly and add the chicken, thyme, lemon zest, and white wine. Cook, stirring occasionally, for 15–20 minutes. Pour in the cream and season with salt and pepper. Continue to cook for about 5 minutes until thickened slightly. Leave to cool.

3 Preheat the oven to 200°C (400°F/Gas 6). Lightly oil the muffin tin. Using the larger biscuit cutter, cut 12 circles from the puff pastry and line the holes in the prepared muffin tin. Spoon the chicken mixture into the pastry shells. With the small biscuit cutter, cut 12 circles from the puff pastry and use them to cover each of the chicken pies. Gently press the edges together to seal. Brush the tops with the egg wash, and bake for 15–20 minutes, until golden brown. Serve hot with a mixed-leaf salad.

Meat and potato pie

Cook this warming winter pie either in a large dish or as individual portions to be eaten with steamed cabbage.

🥣 15 MINS

🍲 1 HR 30 MINS

❄ FREEZABLE

SPECIAL EQUIPMENT

1.2-litre (2-pint) pie dish or 4 small individual pie dishes

SERVES 4

3 potatoes, peeled and cut into bite-sized pieces

675g (1½ lb) braising steak, chopped into bite-sized pieces

1 tbsp olive oil, plus extra for braising

1 onion, finely chopped

1 tbsp plain flour

1 tbsp Worcestershire sauce

450ml (15fl oz) hot beef stock

salt and freshly ground black pepper

300g (10oz) ready-made puff pastry

1 egg, lightly beaten, for egg wash

1 Cook the potatoes in a pan of boiling salted water for 15–20 minutes until soft. Drain and set aside. Put the meat in a large frying pan with a drop of oil, and cook over a high heat for 5–8 minutes until browned all over. Remove with a slotted spoon and set aside.

2 Using the same pan, heat the oil over a low heat. Add the onion and cook gently for about 5 minutes until soft and translucent. Stir in the flour and continue to cook for a further 2 minutes. Increase the heat a little and add the Worcestershire sauce and stock. Bring to the boil, reduce the heat, and return the meat to the pan. Cover and simmer for about 30 minutes, stirring occasionally. Stir through the potato and season well.

3 Meanwhile, preheat the oven to 200°C (400°F/Gas 6). Spoon the meat into the pie dish or small dishes. On a floured work surface, roll out the pastry until 5cm (2in) larger all around than the top of the pie dish. Cut out a strip of pastry about 2.5cm (1in) in from the edge. Wet the edge of the pie dish with a little water; fit the pastry strip all the way around, and press down firmly. Brush the pastry collar with a little of the egg wash, then top with the pastry lid. Trim the excess and pinch the edges to seal. Brush the top of the pie with the egg wash and make 2 slits with a sharp knife to allow steam to escape. Bake for about 30 minutes until puffed and golden. Serve hot.

Steak and wild mushroom pie

This delicious steak pie is both homely and extravagant. Use soaked, dried wild mushrooms if you prefer.

🥣 **55 MINS, PLUS CHILLING**

🍲 **3 HRS**

❄️ **FREEZABLE**

SPECIAL EQUIPMENT

2-litre (3½-pint) pie dish

SERVES 4-6

FOR THE FILLING

salt and freshly ground black pepper

35g (1¼ oz) plain flour

1kg (2¼ lb) braising steak, cut into 2.5cm (1in) cubes

500g (1lb 2oz) wild mushrooms, sliced

4 shallots, finely chopped

900ml (1½ pints) beef stock

handful of parsley leaves, chopped

FOR THE PASTRY

250g (9oz) plain flour, plus extra for dusting

½ tsp fine salt

175g (6oz) unsalted butter, cut into cubes

1 egg, lightly beaten, to glaze

1 Preheat the oven to 180°C (350°F/Gas 4). Season the flour and toss the steak in it to coat. Put the meat, mushrooms, and shallots in a casserole. Add the stock and bring to the boil, stirring. Cover and cook in the oven for 2–2¼ hours until tender.

2 For the pastry, sift the flour and salt into a bowl. Rub in one-third of the butter. Add water to form a dough. Chill for 15 minutes. Roll out to a rectangle on a lightly floured surface. Dot the rest of the butter over two-thirds. Fold the unbuttered third over half the buttered side. Fold again so the butter is enclosed in layers of dough. Turn it over and press the edges to seal. Wrap in cling film and chill for 15 minutes.

3 Roll out and fold as before, make a quarter turn, and seal. Chill for 15 minutes. Repeat 3 more times, chilling between each. Add the parsley to the meat. Spoon it into a 2-litre (3½-pint) pie dish.

4 Increase the heat to 220°C (425°F/Gas 7). Roll out the dough and cut a strip from the edge. Dampen the rim of the dish and press on the strip. Put the rolled-out dough over the pie and seal. Brush with egg. Make a hole in the top. Chill for 15 minutes, then bake for 25–35 minutes.

Cornish pasties

Swede lends sweetness and bulk to these traditional savoury pasties. Worcestershire sauce adds depth of flavour.

🥣 **20 MINS PLUS CHILLING**

🍲 **40-45 MINS**

MAKES 4

100g (3½ oz) lard, chilled and diced

50g (1¾ oz) unsalted butter, chilled and diced

300g (10oz) plain flour, plus extra for dusting

½ tsp salt

1 egg, beaten, for glazing

FOR THE FILLING

250g (9oz) beef skirt, trimmed, cut into 1cm (½ in) cubes

80g (2¾ oz) swede, peeled, cut into 5mm (¼ in) cubes

100g (3½ oz) waxy potatoes, peeled, cut into 5mm (¼ in) cubes

1 large onion, finely chopped

splash of Worcestershire sauce

1 tsp plain flour

sea salt and freshly ground black pepper

1 In a mixing bowl, rub the lard and butter into the flour to resemble fine crumbs. Add the salt and enough cold water to bring the mixture together into a soft dough. Knead briefly on a lightly floured work surface, then wrap in cling film and chill for 1 hour.

2 Preheat the oven to 190°C (375°F/Gas 5). Mix all the filling ingredients in a bowl and season well.

3 Roll the pastry out to a thickness of 5mm (¼ in) on a floured work surface. Using a side plate or saucer, cut 4 circles from the dough. Fold the circles in half, then flatten them out again. Pile one-quarter of the filling into each circle, leaving a 2cm (¾ in) border. Brush the border with a little beaten egg, pull both edges up over the filling, and press together to seal. Crimp the sealed edge with your fingers to form a decorative ridge. Brush beaten egg all over the pasties.

4 Bake in the centre of the oven for 40–45 minutes until golden brown. Allow to cool for at least 15 minutes before eating warm or cold.brushed with a little melted butter. Tuck the edges of the pastry down neatly at the sides, and make sure that the top is well glazed with melted butter. Bake in the oven for 20–30 minutes until the pastry is cooked and golden. Serve hot.

Filo pie with spicy kale and sausage

If you don't have kale to hand, other winter greens work well.

🥣 35-40 MINS

🍲 45-55 MINS

SPECIAL EQUIPMENT

28cm (11in) round springform cake tin

SERVES 6

200g (7oz) unsalted butter

250g (9oz) sausagemeat

3 onions, finely chopped

750g (1lb 10oz) kale, shredded

½ tsp ground allspice

salt and freshly ground black pepper

2 eggs, beaten

500g packet of filo pastry

1 Heat 30g (1oz) of the butter in a pan, add the sausagemeat, and cook, stirring, until brown. Transfer to a bowl, leaving the fat behind. Add the onions to the pan and cook until soft. Add the kale, cover, and cook until wilted. Uncover and cook for 5 minutes, stirring so the moisture evaporates.

2 Return the sausagemeat to the pan with the allspice and stir into the kale mixture. Season to taste. Remove from the heat and let cool completely. Stir in the eggs. Preheat the oven to 180°C (350°F/Gas 4). Melt the remaining butter in a pan; brush the tin with a little butter. Lay a damp tea towel on the work surface. Unroll the filo onto the towel, then using the tin as a guide, cut through the pastry sheets with a 7.5cm (3in) border. Cover the sheets with a second damp towel.

3 Put 1 filo sheet on top of a third damp towel and brush with butter. Transfer to the cake tin, pressing it well into the side. Butter another filo sheet and put it in the tin at a right angle to the first. Continue buttering and layering until half the filo is used, alternating layers at right angles.

4 Spoon the filling into the case. Butter another sheet of filo and cover the filling. Top with the rest of the filo, buttering each sheet. Fold the overhanging dough over the top and drizzle with the remaining butter. Bake the pie in the oven for 45–55 minutes until golden. Let cool slightly, then cut into wedges.

Pea and pancetta tart

The delicate aroma and crisp texture of freshly shelled peas translates into a sweet burst of flavour in this creamy tart.

🥣 10 MINS

🍲 1 HR 15 MINS

❄ FREEZABLE

SPECIAL EQUIPMENT

18cm (7in) round loose-bottomed straight-sided tart tin

ceramic baking beans

SERVES 4-6

300g (10oz) ready-made shortcrust pastry

3 eggs, 1 lightly beaten, for egg wash

1 tbsp olive oil

1 onion, finely chopped

salt and freshly ground black pepper

125g (4½ oz) pancetta, diced

6 sage leaves, roughly chopped

225g (8oz) peas (shelled weight)

150ml (5fl oz) double cream

1 Preheat the oven to 200°C (400°F/Gas 6). Roll out the pastry on a floured work surface to a large circle about 3mm (⅛in) thick and use to line a tart tin, pressing it into the corners. Trim away the excess and prick the bottom with a fork. Line the pastry shell with greaseproof paper and fill with ceramic baking beans. Bake in the oven for 15–20 minutes until the edges are golden. Remove the beans and paper, brush the bottom of the shell with a little of the egg wash, and return to the oven for 2–3 minutes to crisp. Remove from the oven and set aside. Reduce the oven temperature to 180°C (350°F/Gas 4).

2 Meanwhile, heat the oil in a large frying pan over a low heat. Add the onion and a pinch of salt, and cook gently for about 5 minutes until soft and translucent. Add the pancetta and sage, increase the heat a little, and cook for 6–8 minutes until the pancetta is golden and crispy. Stir through the peas, and then season well with salt and pepper.

3 Spoon the onion and pancetta mixture into the pastry shell and level the top. Mix together the cream and eggs, season, and carefully pour the mixture over the filling to cover. Bake in the oven for 20–30 minutes until set and golden. Leave to cool for 10 minutes before releasing from the tin. Serve warm with a tomato salad.

Fish pie

Try to use small, cold-water prawns in this dish, which
are tastier and also less likely to have been farmed.

 20 MINS

30-35 MINS PLUS RESTING

SPECIAL EQUIPMENT

18cm (7in) pie dish

SERVES 4

300g (10oz) skinless salmon fillet

200g (7oz) skinless smoked
   haddock fillet

50g (1¾ oz) unsalted butter

5 tbsp plain flour, plus extra
   for dusting

350ml (12fl oz) whole milk

salt and freshly ground black
   pepper

pinch of grated nutmeg

200g (7oz) cooked prawns, shelled
   and deveined

100g (3½ oz) baby spinach

250g (9oz) shop-bought puff pastry,
   preferably all-butter

1 egg, lightly beaten, for glazing

1 Preheat the oven to 200°C
   (400°F/Gas 6). Poach the
salmon and haddock in simmering
water for 5 minutes. Drain and cool.

2 Melt the butter in a pan.
   Remove from the heat and
whisk in the flour until a paste is
formed. Gradually add the milk,
whisking to avoid any lumps.
Season well and add the nutmeg.
Bring the sauce to the boil, reduce

the heat and cook for 5
minutes, stirring.

3 Flake the fish into a bowl and
   add the prawns. Spread the
uncooked spinach over the top
and pour the hot sauce over it.
Season to taste. When the spinach
has wilted, mix the filling together
and transfer to a 18cm (7in) pie dish.

4 On a floured surface, roll out
   the pastry to a shape bigger
than the pie dish, 3–5mm (⅛–¼ in)
thick. Cut a shape to fit the pie.
Roll some of the trimmings out into
long strips. Brush the rim of the
dish with some egg and press the
pastry strips around the rim.

5 Brush the edging with egg and
   top with the pastry lid. Press
down to seal the lid, and trim off
any overhang. Brush the top with
egg and cut two slits in it. Bake
in the top of the oven for 20–25
minutes until golden, and allow to
rest for 5 minutes before serving.

PREPARE AHEAD

Leave the pie until cold, then
cover, chill overnight, and reheat
the next day. Make sure it is piping
hot to the centre, and cover the top
with foil if the pastry is becoming
too dark.

Crab and prawn saffron tartes

The delicate flavours of crab and prawns balance wonderfully with the assertive pungency and musky taste of saffron.

🥣 **20 MINS**

🍲 **50-65 MINS**

❄️ **FREEZABLE**

SPECIAL EQUIPMENT

15cm (6in) loose-bottomed tart tin

ceramic baking beans

SERVES 2-4

100g (3½ oz) ready-made shortcrust pastry

pinch of saffron

125g (4½ oz) white crab meat

100g (3½ oz) cooked, peeled cold water prawns

200ml (7fl oz) double cream

1 egg

1 tbsp finely chopped tarragon or chervil

sea salt and freshly ground black pepper

1 Roll the pastry out on a floured work surface to a large circle, about 3mm (⅛ in) thick, and use to line the tart tin, pressing it into the corners. Ensure it overlaps the sides by at least 2cm (¾ in). Prick the bottom with a fork. Line with greaseproof paper and fill with ceramic baking beans. Place the tart tin on a baking sheet and bake in the centre of the oven for 20–25 minutes. Remove the beans and paper. Bake for 5 minutes to crisp the bottom. Leave to cool.

2 Splash 1 tbsp boiling water over the saffron in a small bowl to allow the colour to develop. Put the crab meat and prawns in a sieve over a sink and press down to remove any excess water. Toss together and scatter over the pastry base.

3 Whisk the double cream and egg in a jug. Add the herbs, the saffron and its soaking water, and seasoning, and mix well. Put the tart tin on a baking sheet and, with the oven door open, rest it half on, half off the middle oven shelf. Hold the sheet with one hand, pour the cream and egg mix into the tart, and slide it into the oven. Bake for 30–35 minutes until golden. Remove from the oven and leave for 10 minutes. Trim off the overhanging pastry edges with a knife, remove the tart from the tin, and serve warm or cold.

Fish and leek pie

The subtle, sweet flavour of leeks are a great match for fish.

🥣 **15 MINS**

🍲 **50 MINS**

❄️ **FREEZABLE**

SPECIAL EQUIPMENT

1.2-litre (2-pint) pie dish

SERVES 4

1 tbsp olive oil

1 onion, finely chopped

salt and freshly ground black pepper

4 leeks, finely sliced

1 tsp plain flour

150ml (5fl oz) cider

handful of flat-leaf parsley, finely chopped

150ml (5fl oz) double cream

675g (1½ lb) white fish, such as cod or pollack, cut into chunks

300g (10oz) ready-made puff pastry

1 egg, lightly beaten, for egg wash

1 Preheat the oven to 200°C (400°F/Gas 6). Heat the oil in a large frying pan over a low heat. Add the onion and a little salt, and cook gently for about 5 minutes until soft and translucent. Add the leeks and continue to cook gently for about 10 minutes until softened. Remove from the heat, stir in the flour, and add a little of the cider. Return to the heat, pour in the remaining cider, and cook for 5–8 minutes until thickened. Stir through the parsley and cream, then spoon the mixture into a pie dish with the fish. Combine gently, and season well with salt and pepper.

2 Roll out the pastry on a floured work surface, so it is about 5cm (2in) larger all round than the top of the pie dish. Cut out a strip of pastry about 2.5cm (1in) in from the edge to make a collar. Wet the edge of the pie dish with a little water, fit the pastry strip all the way around the edge of the dish, and press down firmly. Brush the pastry collar with a little egg wash, then top with the pastry lid. Trim away the excess and pinch together the edges to seal. Using a sharp knife, make 2 slits in the top to allow steam to escape.

3 Brush the top of the pie with the egg wash and bake in the oven for 20–30 minutes until the pastry is puffed and golden. Serve the pie hot.

Spinach and goat's cheese tart

Fast becoming a modern classic, this dish can be adapted for vegetarians by substituting pancetta with toasted pine nuts.

🥣 **20 MINS**

🍲 **55–1 HR 5 MINS**

❄️ **FREEZABLE**

SPECIAL EQUIPMENT

23cm (9in) loose-bottomed tart tin

ceramic baking beans

SERVES 6–8

150g (5½ oz) ready-made shortcrust pastry

150g (5½ oz) pancetta, diced

1 tbsp olive oil

150g (5½ oz) baby spinach

100g (3½ oz) goat's cheese

sea salt and freshly ground black pepper

300ml (10fl oz) double cream

2 eggs

1 Roll the pastry out on a floured work surface to a large circle, about 3mm (⅛ in) thick, and use to line the tart tin, pressing it into the corners. Ensure it overlaps the sides by at least 2cm (¾ in). Prick the bottom with a fork. Line with greaseproof paper and fill with ceramic baking beans. Place the tart tin on a baking sheet and bake for 20–25 minutes. Remove the beans and paper. Bake for a further 5 minutes to crisp the bottom. Remove and leave to cool.

2 In a frying pan, cook the pancetta in the oil for 5 minutes until golden brown. Add the spinach and cook until it wilts. Drain off any water and allow to cool. Spread the spinach and pancetta mixture over the pastry, cube or crumble the goat's cheese on top, and season.

3 Whisk the cream and eggs in a jug. Place the tart tin on a baking sheet and, with the oven door open, rest it half on, half off the middle oven shelf. Hold the sheet with one hand, pour the cream and egg mix into the tart, and slide it into the oven. Bake for 30–35 minutes or until golden. Remove from the oven and leave for 10 minutes. Trim the overhanging pastry with a knife, remove the tart from the tin, and serve warm or cold.

Creamy spinach tart

Spinach and watercress are a classic spring combination that is enriched here with double cream and a little nutmeg.

🥣 **15 MINS**

🍲 **1 HR**

SPECIAL EQUIPMENT

20cm (8in) round loose-bottomed fluted tart tin

ceramic baking beans

food processor

SERVES 4–6

300g (10oz) ready-made shortcrust pastry

3 eggs, 1 lightly beaten for egg wash

1 tbsp olive oil

1 onion, finely chopped

salt and freshly ground black pepper

2 garlic cloves, grated or finely chopped

450g (1lb) spinach leaves, stalks removed

200g (7oz) watercress

200ml (7fl oz) double cream

pinch of grated nutmeg

1 Preheat the oven to 200°C (400°F/Gas 6). Roll out the pastry on a floured work surface until it is large enough to line the tart tin. Trim away the excess around the edges, line the pastry shell with greaseproof paper, and fill with ceramic baking beans. Bake in the oven for 15–20 minutes until the edges are golden. Remove the beans and greaseproof paper, brush the bottom of the pastry shell with a little of the egg wash, and return to the oven for 2–3 minutes to crisp. Remove from the oven and set aside. Reduce the oven temperature to 180°C (350°F/Gas 4).

2 Heat the oil in a large frying pan over a low heat. Add the onion and a pinch of salt, and sweat gently for about 5 minutes until soft and translucent. Add the garlic and cook for a few more seconds until the garlic turns white. Spoon the mixture into the pastry shell.

3 Put the spinach and atercress in a food processor and pulse a couple of times until broken up, but not mushy. Pour in the cream and the 2 eggs, and pulse again until everything is combined. Season well with salt and pepper, and pulse once more. Carefully pour the mixture into the pastry shell, then sprinkle the nutmeg over, and bake in the oven for 20–30 minutes until set. Leave the tart to cool for 10 minutes before releasing it from the tin.

Filo pie with spinach, ricotta cheese, and pine nuts

The freshest, tenderest spinach is most easily available in spring and is ideal for this subtly flavoured pie.

15 MINS

35 MINS

SPECIAL EQUIPMENT

20cm (8in) round or square loose-bottomed tart tin

SERVES 4

1 tbsp olive oil

1 onion, finely chopped

salt and freshly ground black pepper

2 garlic cloves, grated or finely chopped

550g (1¼ lb) fresh spinach leaves

handful of raisins

75g (2½ oz) pine nuts, toasted

200g (7oz) ricotta cheese

1 egg, lightly beaten

12 sheets filo pastry

30g (1oz) butter, melted

1 Preheat the oven to 180°C (350°F/Gas 4). Heat the oil in a frying pan over a low heat. Add the onion and a little salt, and sweat gently for about 5 minutes until soft and translucent. Add the garlic and cook for a few more seconds until the garlic turns white.

2 Tip in the spinach and cook, stirring, for about 3 minutes until it wilts. Season well with salt and pepper. Remove from the heat, stir through the raisins and pine nuts, and leave to cool. Add the ricotta and beaten egg, and stir well.

3 Lay 2 sheets of filo pastry, one on top of the other, in the cake tin, letting them hang over the edge on two sides. Next, lay 2 more sheets of filo at right angles to the first layer. Continue in this way until you have used 8 sheets for the base of the pie.

4 Spoon the spinach and ricotta mixture into the pie. Fold in the edges of the pastry and top the pie with the remaining 4 sheets of filo pastry, tucking them in neatly. Brush all over with the melted butter and bake in the oven for 20–30 minutes until golden and crisp. Serve warm.

Filo pie with swiss chard, ricotta cheese, and tomatoes

Swiss chard is a relative of beetroot, but its glossy, crinkled leaves and fleshy stems are eaten rather than its roots.

15 MINS

30 MINS

SPECIAL EQUIPMENT

20cm (8in) round, loose-bottomed cake tin

SERVES 4–6

200g (7oz) ricotta cheese

550g (1¼ lb) Swiss chard, chopped

4–6 sun-dried tomatoes in oil, drained and chopped

4 tomatoes, sliced

1 egg

salt and freshly ground black pepper

60g (2oz) butter, melted

8 sheets filo pastry

1 Preheat the oven to 180°C (350°F/Gas 4). In a bowl, mix together the ricotta, Swiss chard, sun-dried and fresh tomatoes, and egg. Season well with salt and pepper.

2 Brush the tin with melted butter. Lay 1 sheet of filo pastry in the tin, letting it hang over the edge on two sides. Lay another sheet at a right angle to the first. Brush with melted butter again. Continue in this way until you have 4 sheets for the base of the pie.

3 Spoon the ricotta mixture into the pie. Fold in the edges of the pastry and top the pie with the remaining 4 sheets of filo pastry, brushing each with a little butter between layers and tucking them in neatly. Brush the top with the remaining butter and bake in the oven for 20–30 minutes until golden and crisp. Serve hot with a salad.

Sweetcorn and pepper filo triangles

Canned or frozen corn doesn't quite compare to the crisp, succulent kernels from a fresh corn cob. Combined with red peppers, they make these pastries crunchy and slightly sweet.

 20 MINS

🍲 20 MINS

❄ FREEZABLE

SERVES 2

1 tbsp olive oil

1 onion, finely chopped

salt and freshly ground black pepper

3 red peppers, deseeded and diced

4 sweetcorn cobs, kernels removed (about 450g/1lb kernels)

175g (6oz) feta cheese, cut into small cubes

200g (7oz) filo pastry

a little butter, melted, plus extra for glazing

1 Preheat the oven to 200°C (400°F/Gas 6). Heat the oil in a large frying pan over a low heat. Add the onion and a little salt, and cook gently for about 5 minutes until soft and translucent. Tip in the peppers and corn, cover, and continue cooking gently for a further 10 minutes until the peppers are soft and the corn is tender, stirring occasionally. Stir through the feta and season well with black pepper.

2 Lay out the filo sheets into four piles of 3 or 4 layers about 30 x 10cm (12 x 4in), brushing each pile with a little melted butter. Divide the pepper mixture between each pile of pastry, spooning it onto the bottom right-hand corner of every one. Fold this corner so that it makes a triangle, then fold the top right-hand corner down. Repeat until you have made 5 folds in all for each one and you end up with 4 large triangles.

3 Brush the triangles all over with a little melted butter and put them on an oiled baking tray. Bake in the oven for about 20 minutes until crisp and golden. Serve hot.

Swiss chard and gruyère cheese tart

Select young, tender stalks of Swiss chard with unblemished dark green leaves. Its slightly bitter, assertive flavour works well with the rich cheese filling of this tart.

🥣 15 MINS

🍲 1 HR

❄ FREEZABLE

SPECIAL EQUIPMENT

23cm (9in) round loose-bottomed fluted tart tin

ceramic baking beans

SERVES 6

300g (10oz) ready-made shortcrust pastry

3 eggs, 1 lightly beaten for egg wash

1 tbsp olive oil

1 onion, finely chopped

salt and freshly ground black pepper

2 garlic cloves, grated or finely chopped

a few sprigs of rosemary, leaves picked and finely chopped

250g (9oz) Swiss chard, stalks trimmed

125g (4½oz) Gruyère cheese, grated

125g (4½oz) feta cheese, cubed

200ml (7fl oz) double cream or whipping cream

1 Preheat the oven to 200°C (400°F/Gas 6). Roll out the pastry on a floured work surface and use to line a tart tin. Trim away the excess, line the pastry shell with greaseproof paper, and fill with ceramic baking beans. Bake in the oven for 15–30 minutes until the edges are golden. Remove the beans and paper, and brush the bottom of the shell with a little of the egg wash. Return to the oven for 1–2 minutes to crisp. Remove from the oven and set aside. Reduce the oven temperature to 180°C (350°F/Gas 4).

2 Heat the oil in a pan over a low heat. Add the onion and salt and sweat gently for about 5 minutes until soft and translucent. Add the garlic and rosemary and cook for a few seconds, then roughly chop the Swiss chard and add to the pan. Stir for about 5 minutes until it wilts.

3 Spoon the onion and chard mixture into the pastry shell. Scatter evenly with the Gruyère and feta cheeses, and season. Mix together the cream and the 2 eggs until well combined, then carefully pour over the tart filling. Bake in the oven for 30–40 minutes until set and golden. Leave to cool for 10 minutes before releasing from the tin. Serve warm.

Squash, thyme, and goat's cheese tart

If you are planning a relaxed weekend lunch with friends, or want a dish to last for a couple of meals, try this tart, which relies on the creamy, buttery flavours of autumnal squash to balance the tang of soft goat's cheese.

15 MINS

1 HR 5 MINS

FREEZABLE

SPECIAL EQUIPMENT

20cm (8in) round loose-bottomed fluted tart tin

ceramic baking beans

SERVES 4-6

300g (10oz) ready-made shortcrust pastry

2 eggs, lightly beaten

1-2 tbsp olive oil

1 onion, finely chopped

salt and freshly ground black pepper

2 garlic cloves, grated or finely chopped

1kg (2¼ lb) butternut squash, peeled, deseeded, and chopped into small cubes

a few sprigs of thyme, leaves picked

125g (4½ oz) soft goat's cheese

200ml (7fl oz) double cream

1 Preheat the oven to 200°C (400°F/Gas 6). Roll out the pastry on a floured work surface to a large circle about 3mm (⅛ in) thick and use to line the tart tin, pressing it into the corners. Trim away the excess and prick the bottom all over with a fork. Line the pastry shell with greaseproof paper and fill the base with ceramic baking beans. Bake the pastry shell in the oven for about 15–20 minutes until the edges of the pastry are golden. Remove the tart tin from the oven, remove the beans and paper, brush the bottom of the pastry shell with a little of the beaten egg, and return to the oven for 2–3 minutes to crisp. Remove from the oven once again and set aside. Reduce the oven temperature to 180°C (350°F/Gas 4).

2 Meanwhile, heat 1 tbsp of the oil in a large frying pan over a low heat. Add the onion and a little salt, and cook gently for about 5 minutes until soft and translucent. Add the garlic, squash, and half of the thyme leaves, and continue cooking over a low heat for 10–15 minutes until the squash softens and begins to turn golden. You may have to add a little more oil.

3 Spoon the squash and onion mixture into the pastry shell, then crumble over the goat's cheese. Mix the cream with the remaining beaten egg and season well with salt and pepper. Pour the cream mixture over the tart filling, then sprinkle with the remaining thyme leaves. Bake in the oven for 20–25 minutes until the tart is puffed and set. Leave to cool for at least 10 minutes before releasing it from the tin. Serve the tart while still warm with a rocket salad.

Artichoke, green olive, and feta tart

There is a nice Mediterranean touch to this tart with salty olives and feta cheese counterbalancing the sweet artichoke.

 15 MINS

1 HR

SPECIAL EQUIPMENT

35 x 12cm (14 x 5in) loose-bottomed fluted tart tin

ceramic baking beans

SERVES 6

250g (9oz) ready-made shortcrust pastry

3 eggs, 1 lightly beaten, for egg wash

1 tbsp olive oil

1 onion, finely chopped

2 garlic cloves, grated or finely chopped

5 large cooked artichoke hearts

12 green olives, pitted

175g (6oz) feta cheese, cubed

a few sprigs of thyme, leaves picked

200ml (7fl oz) double cream

salt and freshly ground black pepper

1 Preheat the oven to 200°C (400°F/Gas 6). Roll out the pastry on a floured work surface and use it to line the tart tin. Trim away the excess, then line the pastry shell with greaseproof paper and fill with ceramic baking beans. Bake in the oven for 15–20 minutes until the edges are golden. Remove the beans and paper, brush the bottom of the shell with a little of the egg wash, and return to the oven for 2–3 minutes to crisp. Remove from the oven and set aside. Reduce the oven temperature to 180°C (350°F/Gas 4).

2 Heat the oil in a pan over a low heat, add the onion, and cook for about 5 minutes until soft. Add the garlic and cook for a few more seconds. Spoon the onion mixture evenly over the bottom of the tart shell. Arrange the artichokes and olives over the top and sprinkle with the feta and thyme leaves.

3 Mix together the cream, 2 eggs, and seasoning. Pour over the tart filling. Bake in the oven for 25–35 minutes until set, puffed, and golden. Leave to cool for about 10 minutes before releasing from the tin. Serve warm, or at room temperature, with a rocket and tomato salad.

Broccoli and mushroom quiche

Both broccoli stalks and florets earn a starring role in this lovely autumnal quiche flavoured with garlic, Parmesan, and nutmeg.

 20 MINS

30-35 MINS

SPECIAL EQUIPMENT

25cm (10in) round loose-bottomed fluted flan tin

ceramic baking beans

SERVES 6-8

300g (10oz) ready-made shortcrust pastry

1–2 heads of broccoli, total weight about 500g (1lb 2oz)

salt and freshly ground black pepper

30g (1oz) butter

175g (6oz) mushrooms, sliced

2 garlic cloves, finely chopped

3 eggs, plus 2 egg yolks

375ml (13fl oz) milk

250ml (9fl oz) double cream

60g (2oz) Parmesan cheese, grated

grated nutmeg

1 Preheat the oven to 220°C (425°F/Gas 7). Lightly flour a work surface and roll out the pastry to a 30cm (12in) round. Use to line the tin, pressing it into the corners. Trim away the excess and prick the bottom all over with a fork. Line the pastry shell with greaseproof paper and fill with ceramic baking beans. Bake in the oven for 12–15 minutes until the edges are golden. Remove the beans and paper and return to the oven for 2–3 minutes to crisp. Remove from the oven and set aside. Reduce the oven temperature to 190°C (375°F/Gas 5).

2 Cut the florets from the broccoli stalk, then slice the stalk lengthways into sticks. Half-fill a saucepan with water and bring to the boil. Add salt, then the broccoli. Cook until just tender; it should take only about 3–5 minutes. Drain and set aside.

3 Melt the butter in a frying pan, add the mushrooms and garlic, and sauté until the mushrooms have first given out all their liquid, and then all that liquid has evaporated.

4 Whisk together the eggs, egg yolks, milk, cream, grated cheese, salt, pepper, and a pinch of nutmeg. Spread the mushrooms in the pastry shell. Arrange the broccoli on top. Ladle the cheese custard over to fill almost to the rim. Bake for 30–35 minutes, until browned and the custard has a slight wobble in the centre when shaken. Serve hot or at room temperature.

Mushroom and ricotta pies with red pepper pesto

For a slightly sweeter taste and a paler colour, you can use orange or yellow peppers for the pesto.

🥄 25 MINS

🍲 45 MINS

❄ FREEZABLE

SPECIAL EQUIPMENT

blender or food processor

SERVES 4

13 tbsp olive oil

150g (5½ oz) button mushrooms, halved

150g (5½ oz) mixed wild mushrooms

1 leek, white part only, finely sliced

2 sheets ready-rolled puff pastry

200g (7oz) ricotta cheese

1 egg yolk, lightly beaten

FOR THE RED PEPPER PESTO

2 tbsp olive oil

1 onion, sliced

2 red peppers, sliced

2 garlic cloves, crushed

zest and juice of 1 small lemon

salt and freshly ground black pepper

1 Preheat the oven to 200°C (400°F/Gas 6) and line a baking tray with baking parchment. To make the red pepper pesto, heat the oil in a heavy-based frying pan over a low heat. Add the onion and sweat gently for a few minutes until translucent. Tip in the peppers and sweat for a further 10–15 minutes until soft. Transfer the mixture to a blender or food processor. Add the garlic and lemon zest and juice, and blitz to a chunky purée. Season and set aside.

2 Heat the 3 tbsp oil in a large heavy-based frying pan over a medium heat. Add the mushrooms and leek, and sauté, stirring, for 5 minutes until the mushrooms have browned. Set aside.

3 Cut each pastry sheet into quarters. Using a sharp knife, cut diagonal slashes across the surface of half the pastry squares, taking care not to slice all the way through. Spread the ricotta over the surface of the uncut squares, leaving a 1cm (½ in) border of pastry round the edges. Spoon the mushroom and leek mixture evenly over the ricotta, then lay the slit pastry squares evenly over the top of the mushrooms. Pinch and twist together the corners of the pies and brush the tops with the egg yolk.

4 Place the pies on the baking tray and bake in the oven for 25 minutes until golden brown. Serve with the red pepper pesto and a leafy green salad.

Mixed mushroom and walnut tart

Autumn is the time when fresh wild mushrooms are in abundance and you will have a choice of varieties such as ceps, field mushrooms, and golden chanterelles.

🥄 15 MINS

🍲 1 HR

❄ FREEZABLE

SPECIAL EQUIPMENT

12 x 35cm (5 x 14in) rectangular loose-bottomed fluted tart tin

ceramic baking beans

SERVES 6

250g (9oz) ready-made shortcrust pastry

2 eggs, plus 1 lightly beaten

3-4 tbsp olive oil

140g (5oz) mixed wild mushrooms, roughly chopped

200g (7oz) chestnut mushrooms, roughly chopped

3 garlic cloves, grated or finely chopped

50g (1¾ oz) walnuts, roughly chopped

salt and freshly ground black pepper

2 handfuls of spinach leaves, roughly chopped

200ml (7fl oz) double cream

1 Preheat the oven to 200°C (400°F/Gas 6). Roll out the pastry on a floured work surface and use to line the tart tin. Trim away the excess, line the pastry shell with greaseproof paper, and fill with ceramic baking beans. Bake in the oven for 15–20 minutes until the edges are golden. Remove the beans and paper, brush the bottom of the shell with a little of the beaten egg, and return to the oven for 2–3 minutes to crisp. Remove from the oven and set aside. Reduce the oven temperature to 180°C (350°F/Gas 4).

2 Heat the oil in a large, deep frying pan over a low heat. Add the mushrooms, garlic, and walnuts, and season well with salt and pepper. Cook, stirring occasionally, for about 10 minutes until the mushrooms release their juices. Tip in the spinach and cook, stirring, for a further 5 minutes until just wilted. Spoon the mixture into the pastry shell.

3 Mix together the cream and eggs and season well. Carefully pour the cream mixture over the mushroom filling. Sprinkle with a pinch of black pepper and bake in the oven for 15–20 minutes until set. Leave to cool for 10 minutes before releasing from the tin. Serve hot or cold.

Flemish vegetable tart

A quick brioche dough makes a sumptuous crust for this unusual vegetable tart. You can choose to cook the tart in a frying pan, if you like, for a more rustic effect. Don't be worried about making brioche: this version is very easy indeed, and has the advantage that it can be made the day ahead and refrigerated, wrapped in cling film, overnight.

🥣 **50-55 MINS PLUS RISING**

🍲 **40-50 MINS**

SPECIAL EQUIPMENT

30cm (12in) flan dish

SERVES 8

1½ tsp dried yeast

250g (9oz) strong plain flour, more if needed

salt and freshly ground black pepper

7 eggs

215g (7½oz) unsalted butter, softened

4 carrots, cut in julienne strips

500g (1lb 2oz) mushrooms, stalks removed and caps thinly sliced

2 turnips, cut in julienne strips

8-10 spring onions, trimmed and finely sliced

250ml (9fl oz) double cream

¼ tsp grated nutmeg

1 For the dough, sprinkle the yeast over 2 tbsp lukewarm water in a bowl and let stand for 5 minutes. Oil a medium bowl. Sift the flour on to a work surface with 1 tsp salt. Make a well in the centre and add the yeast and 3 eggs. Work the ingredients until thoroughly mixed. Draw in the flour and work into the other ingredients with your fingertips to form a smooth dough; add more flour if it is sticky.

2 Place the dough on a floured surface and knead for about 10 minutes, lifting it up and throwing it down until it is very elastic. Work in more flour as necessary, so it is slightly sticky but peels easily from the work surface. Add 125g (4½ oz) of the butter, and pinch and squeeze to mix it into the dough. Knead for 3–5 minutes, until smooth again. Shape into a ball and put into the oiled bowl. Cover with cling film and chill for about 1 hour.

3 Melt the remaining butter in a pan. Add the carrots and cook gently for about 5 minutes, stirring occasionally. Add the mushrooms and turnips, and season with salt and pepper. Press buttered foil over the vegetables, cover with a lid, and cook for about 10 minutes until tender, stirring occasionally. Remove from the heat, add the spring onions, and season.

4 Heat the oven to 200°C (400°F/Gas 6) and butter the flan dish. Place the dough on a floured surface and lightly knead it to knock out the air. Roll out to a round 7.5cm (3in) larger than the dish. Line the dish and spread the vegetable mixture in the case. Whisk together the cream, salt, pepper, and nutmeg with the remaining eggs, and pour over the vegetables.

5 Fold the top edge of the dough rim over the filling to form a border. Let rise in a warm place for 20–30 minutes until puffed up. Bake for 40–50 minutes until the brioche case is very brown and the custard set but retaining a slight wobble. Serve hot or at room temperature.

Asparagus and herb tart

The asparagus laid in neat rows in this rectangular tart makes for a fun and unusual piece of presentation.

 15 MINS

1 HR

SPECIAL EQUIPMENT

18 x 30cm (7 x 12in) rectangular loose-bottomed fluted tart tin

ceramic baking beans

SERVES 6–8

250g (9oz) ready-made shortcrust pastry

3 eggs, 1 lightly beaten, for egg wash

350g (12oz) asparagus spears, trimmed

1 tbsp olive oil

bunch of spring onions, trimmed and finely chopped

handful of mint leaves, finely chopped

salt and freshly ground black pepper

125g (4½ oz) Cheddar cheese, grated

200ml (7fl oz) double cream

pinch of grated nutmeg

1 Preheat the oven to 200°C (400°F/Gas 6). Roll out the pastry on a floured work surface, and use to line the tart tin. Trim the excess, line the pastry shell with greaseproof paper, and fill with ceramic baking beans. Bake for 15–20 minutes until the edges are golden. Remove the beans and paper, and brush egg wash over the bottom of the shell. Return to the oven for 2–3 minutes to crisp. Remove from the oven and set aside. Reduce the oven temperature to 180°C (350°F/Gas 4).

2 Cook the asparagus spears in boiling salted water for 2–4 minutes, or until soft. Drain, refresh in cold water, and drain again. Heat the oil in a pan over a low heat. Add the spring onions, and sweat for 2 minutes. Remove from the pan with a slotted spoon, and scatter over the bottom of the pastry shell. Arrange the asparagus on top. Scatter over the mint, add seasoning, and sprinkle over the cheese. Mix the cream, 2 eggs, and the nutmeg. Pour the mixture over the tart, and bake for 30–40 minutes until set and golden. Leave in the tin for 10 minutes before serving with a tomato salad.

Roasted red pepper tart

Red pesto and mascarpone add depth to this sweet pepper filling. Preheat a baking sheet in the oven and place the tart tin on top to achieve a really crisp pastry base.

🥣 **15 MINS**

🍲 **1 HR**

❄️ **FREEZABLE**

SPECIAL EQUIPMENT

23cm (9in) square loose-bottomed fluted tart tin

ceramic baking beans

food processor

SERVES 6–8

4 large red peppers

1 tbsp olive oil

300g (10oz) ready-made shortcrust pastry

3 eggs, 1 lightly beaten for egg wash

1 tbsp mascarpone

handful of basil leaves, plus extra to garnish

salt and freshly ground black pepper

1 tsp red pesto

1 Preheat the oven to 200°C (400°F/Gas 6). Put the peppers in a roasting tin. Using your hands, smear each one with the oil. Roast in the oven for about 20 minutes until lightly charred. Transfer to a plastic bag and leave until cool enough to handle, before skinning and deseeding.

2 Meanwhile, roll out the pastry on a floured work surface and use to line a tart tin. Trim away the excess, line the pastry shell with greaseproof paper, and fill with ceramic baking beans. Bake in the oven for 15–20 minutes until the edges are golden. Remove the beans and paper, brush the bottom of the shell with the extra egg wash, and return to the oven for 2–3 minutes to crisp. Remove from the oven and set aside. Reduce the oven temperature to 180°C (350°F/Gas 4).

3 Put the roasted peppers, the 2 eggs, mascarpone, and the basil leaves in a food processor and blitz until combined. Season well with salt and pepper. Spread the pesto evenly over the bottom of the pastry shell, then carefully pour in the pepper mixture. Bake in the oven for 25–35 minutes until set. Leave to cool for 10 minutes before releasing from the tin. Garnish with extra basil leaves and serve with a wild rocket and fennel salad.

Curried vegetable pies

A summer vegetable medley of young carrots, courgettes, and spring onions are combined with potatoes in these pies. Their handy size makes them easy to take on a picnic or for a lunchtime snack. Depending on how hot you like your curry, you can buy curry pastes ranging from mild to extra hot. The pastes are a mixture of ground herbs and spices pounded into a vegetable oil.

🥄 **1 MINS**

🍲 **45 MINS**

❄️ **FREEZABLE**

SPECIAL EQUIPMENT

15cm (6in) round biscuit cutter

MAKES 4

1 carrot, diced

2 potatoes, peeled and finely diced

salt and freshly ground black pepper

450g (1lb) ready-made shortcrust pastry

1 egg, lightly beaten, for egg wash

1 tbsp curry paste

2 tbsp Greek-style yogurt

1 garlic clove, grated or finely chopped

2.5cm (1in) piece of fresh root ginger, peeled and finely chopped

1 courgette, diced

2 spring onions, trimmed and finely sliced

handful of coriander, finely chopped

juice of ½ lemon

1 Preheat the oven to 200°C (400°F/Gas 6). Cook the carrot and potatoes in a pan of salted water for about 15 minutes until soft; drain well.

2 Roll out the pastry on a floured work surface, then cut out 4 circles using the biscuit cutter. Put the pastry rounds on a baking tray and brush the edges with a little of the egg wash.

3 Put the carrot and potatoes in a bowl and gently mix with the curry paste and yogurt. Add the garlic, ginger, courgette, spring onions, coriander, and lemon juice, and season well with salt and pepper. Stir in gently until well mixed.

4 Divide the vegetable mixture evenly among the pastry circles, spooning it into the centre of each one. Fold over the pastry to make a half-moon shape, and pinch the edges together to seal. Transfer to a baking sheet. Using a sharp knife, make 2 or 3 slashes in the top of each pie, then brush all over with the remaining egg wash. Bake in the oven for 20–30 minutes until golden. Serve hot or cold.

Caramelized shallot tart

The allium family is indispensible to most cooks, yet we rarely find ways of allowing onions and shallots to take centre stage. This simple recipe gives shallots a starring role.

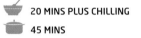 20 MINS PLUS CHILLING

45 MINS

SPECIAL EQUIPMENT

food processor

SERVES 4-6

25g (scant 1oz) butter

2 tbsp extra virgin olive oil

400g (14oz) shallots, split in half
   lengthways

2 tbsp balsamic vinegar

a few sprigs of thyme

For the pastry

150g (5½ oz) plain flour

sea salt

75g (2½ oz) butter

1 For the pastry, combine the flour, a pinch of sea salt, and the butter in a food processor and mix to form fine breadcrumbs. With the motor running, add cold water, 1 tbsp at a time, until the pastry starts to stick together. Form the pastry into a ball, wrap it in cling film, and leave it in the fridge to chill for 30 minutes.

2 Preheat the oven to 200°C (400°F/Gas 6). In a large, ovenproof frying pan, melt the butter with the oil over a medium heat. Put the shallots in, cut-side down, and cook very gently for 10 minutes until they are browned. Turn them over and cook for another 5 minutes. Add the balsamic vinegar and 2 tbsp water, then remove from the heat. Tuck the sprigs of thyme between the shallots.

3 Roll out the pastry into a circle a little larger than the frying pan. Lay the pastry over the shallots, trim, and tuck it in. Transfer the pan to the oven and cook for 30 minutes until the pastry is golden brown.

4 Remove the pan from the oven and bang it gently to loosen the shallots. Run a knife around the edges of the pastry, then put a large plate over the pan and quickly turn it over. Serve warm with a green salad.

Tomato and harissa tart

Harissa paste is a thick chilli sauce that includes chilli peppers as well as garlic, coriander, chilli powder, and caraway blended with olive oil. Use as much of the paste as suits your taste.

 10 MINS

15 MINS

SERVES 6

400g (14oz) ready-made
   puff pastry

2 tbsp red pepper pesto

6 tomatoes, halved

2-3 tbsp harissa paste

1 tbsp olive oil

a few sprigs of thyme, leaves picked

1 Preheat the oven to 200°C (400°F/Gas 6). Roll out the pastry on a floured work surface into a large rectangle or square. Lay on a baking tray, then use a sharp knife to score a border about 5cm (2in) in from the edges all the way around, being careful not to cut all the way through the pastry. Next, using the back of the knife, score the pastry around the outer edges – this will help it to puff up.

2 Working inside the border, smother the pastry with the pesto. Arrange the tomatoes on top, cut-side up. Mix the harissa paste with the oil and drizzle over the tomatoes. Scatter over the thyme leaves.

3 Bake in the oven for about 15 minutes until the pastry is cooked and golden. Serve hot.

Onion tart

An onion tart is very simple fare made with a minimal number of ingredients. Don't hold back on the seasoning, which helps to bring out the flavour of the onions even more. The addition of paprika in this version brings added colour as well as flavour.

🥣 **15 MINS**

🍲 **55 MINS**

❄️ **FREEZABLE**

SPECIAL EQUIPMENT

20cm (8in) round fluted tart tin

ceramic baking beans

SERVES 6

1 tbsp olive oil

4 onions, sliced

1 tbsp plain flour

300ml (10fl oz) milk

2 tsp mild paprika

salt and freshly ground black pepper

300g (10oz) ready-made shortcrust pastry

1 egg, lightly beaten, for egg wash

1 Preheat the oven to 200°C (400°F/Gas 6). Heat the oil in a large, non-stick, heavy-based pan over a low heat. Add the onions and sweat very gently for about 15 minutes until soft and translucent. Keep stirring throughout, so that the onions don't stick or brown.

2 Remove from the heat and stir in the flour with a wooden spoon. Add a little of the milk and stir until combined. Return the pan to the heat and keep adding the milk, slowly and gradually, stirring continuously as the mixture thickens. Add 1 tsp of the paprika and season well with salt and pepper. Remove from the heat and set aside.

3 Roll out the pastry on a floured work surface and use to line the tart tin. Trim away any excess, line the pastry shell with greaseproof paper, and fill with the ceramic baking beans. Bake in the oven for 15–20 minutes until the edges of the pastry are golden. Remove the beans and paper, brush the bottom of the shell with a little of the egg wash, and return to the oven for a couple of minutes to crisp. Reduce the oven temperature to 180°C (350°F/Gas 4).

4 Carefully spoon the onion mixture into the pastry shell and sprinkle with the remaining paprika. Return the pie to the oven and bake for 15–20 minutes until lightly golden. Serve warm with a green salad.

Strawberry-raspberry tart

This heavenly summer tart is nothing more than fresh fruits, whipped cream, and hazelnuts on a pastry base.

🥣 **35-40 MINS PLUS CHILLING**

🍲 **30-35 MINS**

SPECIAL EQUIPMENT

23-25cm (9-10in) round springform fluted tart tin

electric hand whisk

food processor

SERVES 6-8

140g (5oz) hazelnuts

melted butter, for brushing

500g (1lb 2oz) ready-made sweet shortcrust pastry

250ml (9fl oz) double cream

3-4 tbsp icing sugar, plus more to dust

2 tbsp Marsala wine

125g (4½ oz) raspberries

300g (10oz) strawberries, hulled and cut in half or into quarters if large

1 Preheat the oven to 180°C (350°F/Gas 4). Spread the nuts on a baking sheet. Toast for 8–10 minutes until lightly browned. Rub in a clean tea towel to remove the skins. Leave to cool, roughly chop 60g (2oz) of the nuts and reserve, and blitz the rest to a powder in a food processor.

2 Leave the oven on. Brush the tart tin with melted butter. Roll out the pastry on a floured work surface to a circle larger than the tin and about 3mm (⅛in) thick, and use it to line the tin, pressing it into the corners. Chill for at least 15 minutes in the fridge until firm. Bake for 30–35 minutes until golden brown and shrinking slightly from the tin. Cool, then remove the sides of the tin.

3 Pour the cream into a mixing bowl and whisk with an electric hand whisk until soft peaks form. Add the ground hazelnuts, icing sugar, and Marsala wine. Continue whisking until stiff peaks form.

4 Ensuring the pastry is completely cold, spread two-thirds of the Marsala and hazelnut whipped cream evenly over the pastry shell, just to the edge. Arrange most of the fruit evenly over the cream. Top with the remaining Marsala cream, then scatter with the remaining fruits and the reserved chopped nuts. Chill in the fridge, then dust with icing sugar before serving.

Mixed berry flan

This is a truly instant dessert, comprising a ready-made sponge base filled with soft ice cream, juicy raspberries, strawberries, blackberries, and redcurrants.

🥣 **10 MINS**

SERVES 6

3-4 scoops soft chocolate ice cream

3-4 scoops soft vanilla ice cream

20cm (8in) ready-made round plain sponge base

500g (1lb 2oz) mixed summer berries, such as raspberries, blackberries, strawberries (hulled and quartered), and redcurrants

drizzle of crème de cassis, or other liqueur of your choice (optional)

1 Spoon the ice cream onto the sponge base, arranging it in a small mound in the centre of the base, if you like, then pile the fruit on top and around the edges of the base.

2 Drizzle over the crème de cassis, or other liqueur (if using), and serve the flan immediately.

Gooseberry tart

Tangy gooseberries quiver in smooth, just-set custard, in a light sweet pastry crust for a sublime seasonal treat.

🥣 **30 MINS PLUS CHILLING**

🍲 **1 HR**

SPECIAL EQUIPMENT

electric hand whisk

25cm (10in) round loose-bottomed fluted tart tin

ceramic baking beans

SERVES 6-8

175g (6oz) plain flour

75g (2½ oz) butter

75g (2½ oz) caster sugar

2 egg yolks, plus 2 eggs

250ml (9fl oz) double cream

400g (14oz) gooseberries, topped and tailed

thick cream, to serve (optional)

1 In a large bowl, rub together the flour and butter until they resemble crumbs. Stir in 25g (scant 1oz) of the sugar, add the egg yolks, then bring the ingredients together to form a dough. Wrap in cling film and chill for 30 minutes.

2 Preheat the oven to 180°C (350°F/Gas 4). To make the custard, put the double cream, eggs, and the remaining sugar in a mixing bowl and whisk together with an electric hand whisk. Then leave to chill in the fridge.

3 Roll out the pastry on a floured work surface to a circle a little larger than the tin. Line the tin with the pastry, pressing it into the corners. Prick the bottom with a fork. Line the pastry shell with greaseproof paper and fill with baking beans. Bake in the oven for 20 minutes. Remove the beans and paper and return to the oven for 5 minutes more to crisp. Remove from the oven and set aside.

4 Arrange a layer of gooseberries over the base of the pastry shell. Pour the custard over and bake for 35 minutes until set and golden. Allow to cool slightly before removing from the tin and serving with thick cream, if you like.

Raspberry tart with chocolate cream

A chocolate-lined pastry is a perfect partner for raspberries.

🥣 **40 MINS PLUS CHILLING**

🍲 **20-25 MINS**

SPECIAL EQUIPMENT

23cm (9in) round loose-bottomed fluted tart tin

ceramic baking beans

SERVES 6-8

125g (4½ oz) plain flour

20g (¾ oz) cocoa powder

100g (3½ oz) unsalted butter, diced

150g (5½ oz) caster sugar

1 egg yolk, plus 2 eggs

1½ tsp vanilla extract

50g (1¾ oz) cornflour, sifted

450ml (15fl oz) whole milk

175g (6oz) dark chocolate, in pieces

400g (14oz) raspberries

1 Rub together the flour, cocoa, and butter to resemble breadcrumbs. Stir in 50g (1¾ oz) of the sugar. Beat the egg yolk with ½ tsp of the vanilla and add to the flour mixture, bringing it together to form a soft dough. Add a little extra water if it seems too dry. Wrap in cling film and chill for 1 hour.

2 Preheat the oven to 180°C (350°F/Gas 4). Roll the pastry out on a floured surface to 3mm (⅛ in) thick and use to line the tin, pressing it into the corners and overlapping the edges by 2cm (¾ in). Prick the bottom with a fork. Line the shell with greaseproof paper and fill with baking beans. Place on a baking sheet and bake for 20 minutes. Remove the beans and paper, and return to the oven for 5 minutes. Then trim the overlapping pastry.

3 Beat 100g (3½ oz) of the sugar, the eggs, cornflour, and 1 tsp of the vanilla in a bowl. In a pan, bring the milk and 100g (3½ oz) of the chocolate to the boil, whisking all the time. Take off the heat as it starts to bubble. Pour onto the egg mixture, whisking. Return to the cleaned-out pan and bring to the boil over a medium heat, whisking. Reduce the heat to its lowest when it thickens and cook for 2–3 minutes, whisking. Pour into a bowl, cover with cling film, and cool.

4 Melt the remaining chocolate in a bowl set over a pan of simmering water, and brush around the inside of the tart case. Leave to set. Beat the chocolate cream with a wooden spoon and pour into the case. Arrange the raspberries on top, remove from the tin, and serve dusted with icing sugar.

Fig and mulled wine tart

With their delicate flavour, figs call for the simplest treatment.

 25-30 MINS PLUS CHILLING

15-20 MINS

SPECIAL EQUIPMENT

25cm (10in) round loose-bottomed fluted tart tin

SERVES 6-8

375g (13oz) ready-made sweet shortcrust pastry

250ml (9fl oz) milk

½ vanilla pod, split lengthways

3 egg yolks

3 tbsp caster sugar

2 tbsp flour

10g (¼ oz) unsalted butter

90ml (3fl oz) double cream, whipped

pared zest of 1 orange

pared zest of 1 lemon

1 nutmeg, crushed

100g (3½ oz) caster sugar

5cm (2in) piece of cinnamon stick

2 whole cloves

500ml (16fl oz) dry red wine

500g (1lb 2oz) figs, skins pricked

1 Preheat the oven to 190°C (375°F/Gas 5). Butter the tart tin. Roll out the pastry on a floured surface and use to line the tin. Chill for 15 minutes, then bake for 15–20 minutes until golden. Put on a wire rack, loosen the tin, and let the pastry cool.

2 For the pastry cream, bring the milk and vanilla to the boil in a pan. Remove from the heat. In a bowl, whisk the egg yolks and sugar until thick. Stir in the flour and then the hot milk. Return to the pan. Bring to the boil, whisking, until thickened. Reduce the heat and cook, whisking, for about 2 minutes, until it softens. Remove from the heat, discard the vanilla pod, and transfer to a bowl. Rub the butter over and chill for 30 minutes. Fold in the whipped cream.

3 Put the zest and nutmeg into a pan with the sugar, spices, and wine. Heat, stirring, to dissolve the sugar. Bring to the boil, then add the figs. Poach for 3–5 minutes, until the figs are tender. Remove the figs and set aside. Simmer the syrup until reduced to about 120ml (4fl oz). Strain and cool. Halve the figs, then cut them nearly through into quarters. Spread the pastry cream over the chilled pastry shell and arrange the figs on top. Spoon 1–2 tbsp syrup over the figs. Just before serving, spoon over the rest.

Apricot clafoutis

A clafoutis is a baked French dessert with a flan-like batter covering fresh fruit. Usually black cherries, here apricots are used. It can be enjoyed warm or at room temperature.

10 MINS

35 MINS

SPECIAL EQUIPMENT

1.2-litre (2-pint) shallow ovenproof dish

SERVES 4

250g (9oz) ripe apricots, halved and stoned

1 egg, plus 1 egg yolk

25g (scant 1oz) plain flour

50g (1¾ oz) caster sugar

150ml (5fl oz) double cream

¼ tsp vanilla extract

thick cream or crème fraîche, to serve (optional)

1 Preheat the oven to 200°C (400°F/Gas 6). Lightly butter the ovenproof dish. Place the apricots cut-side down in a single layer in the dish; there should be a small amount of space between them.

2 In a bowl, whisk together the egg, egg yolk, and the flour. Whisk in the sugar. Finally, add the cream and vanilla extract, and whisk thoroughly to form a smooth custard-like batter.

3 Pour the batter around the apricots, so the tops of a few are just visible. Bake on the top shelf of the oven for 35 minutes until puffed up and golden brown in places. Remove and let cool for at least 15 minutes. Serve warm, with thick cream or crème fraîche, if using.

Chocolate and pear tartlets

For the best result, ensure your pears are fully ripe and juicy.

🥣 30-35 MINS

🍲 25-30 MINS

SPECIAL EQUIPMENT

8 x 10cm (4in) round fluted tartlet tins

MAKES 8

melted butter, for greasing

350g (12oz) ready-made sweet shortcrust pastry

150g (5½ oz) plain chocolate, finely chopped

1 egg

125ml (4½ fl oz) single cream

2 large ripe pears

1-2 tbsp caster sugar, to sprinkle

1 Brush the insides of the tartlet tins with melted butter. Group 4 of the tartlet tins together with their edges nearly touching. Sprinkle a work surface lightly with flour. Divide the pastry in half and roll 1 piece out to 3mm (⅛ in) thick. Roll the pastry loosely round the rolling pin and drape it over the 4 tins to cover them.

2 Tear off a small piece of pastry from the edge, form it into a ball, dip it in flour, and use it to push the pastry into the tins. Roll the rolling pin over the tops of the tins to cut off excess pastry. Roll up the trimmings with the other piece of pastry and repeat with the remaining tins.

3 Preheat the oven to 200°C (400°F/Gas 6). Heat a baking sheet on a shelf near the bottom of the oven. Sprinkle the chocolate into each tartlet shell.

4 To make the custard, whisk the egg and cream until thoroughly mixed. For an extra-smooth custard, run the mixture through a sieve. Spoon 2-3 tbsp of the custard over the chocolate in each tartlet shell.

5 Peel the pears, cut them in half, and remove the cores. Cut each pear half into very thin slices widthways. Arrange the slices on the custard so they overlap. Press them down very lightly into the custard, so it will bake up around the fruit, then sprinkle each tartlet evenly with the sugar.

6 Place the tartlet tins on the heated baking sheet. Bake for 10 minutes, then reduce the heat to 180°C (350°F/Gas 4) and continue baking for 15–20 minutes until the pastry is golden and the custard has set.

7 Leave the tartlets to cool slightly. Once cool enough to handle, carefully unmould them and place the tartlets on individual plates to serve.

Apple tart

When Bramley apples are in season, it is the classic apple tart that comes to mind. Slice the apples thinly for a pretty effect.

🥣 15 MINS

🍲 25 MINS

❄️ FREEZABLE

SPECIAL EQUIPMENT

20cm (8in) round fluted tart tin

ceramic baking beans

SERVES 6

225g (8oz) ready-made sweet shortcrust pastry

1 egg, beaten

4 Bramley apples, peeled, cored, and thinly sliced

2-3 tbsp golden caster sugar

knob of butter

1 Preheat the oven to 220°C (425°F/Gas 7). On a lightly floured surface, roll the pastry out as thinly as you can. Use to line the tart tin, pressing it into the corners. Trim away the excess and prick the bottom all over with a fork. Line the pastry shell with greaseproof paper and fill with ceramic baking beans. Bake in the oven for 10 minutes, or until the edges are golden. Remove the beans and paper, brush the bottom of the shell with a little of the egg wash, and return to the oven for 2–3 minutes to crisp. Remove from the oven and set aside. Allow the tart case to cool, but leave the oven on.

2 Arrange the apple slices in the tart case in a neat, overlapping design. Sprinkle with the sugar and dot with the butter. Bake in the oven for 10–15 minutes, or until the apples begin to caramelize and the pastry is golden. Leave to cool. Remove from the tin and place on a plate to serve.

Almond and raspberry lattice tart

This is the Viennese speciality Linzertorte made with almond lattice pastry.

30-35 MINS PLUS CHILLING

40-45 MINS

SPECIAL EQUIPMENT

23cm (9in) round loose-bottomed
   fluted tart tin

food processor

fluted pastry wheel (optional)

SERVES 6-8

125g (4½ oz) plain flour

pinch of ground cloves

½ tsp ground cinnamon

175g (6oz) ground almonds

125g (4½ oz) unsalted butter,
   softened and diced

1 egg yolk

100g (3½ oz) caster sugar

salt

grated zest of 1 lemon, and juice
   of ½ lemon

FOR THE FILLING

125g (4½ oz) caster sugar

375g (13oz) raspberries

1-2 tbsp icing sugar, for dusting

1 Sift the flour into a bowl. Mix
in the cloves, cinnamon, and
almonds, and make a well in
the centre.

2 In a separate bowl and using
your fingers, mix together the
butter, yolk, sugar, ¼ tsp salt, and
lemon zest and juice. Place in the
well. Then draw in the flour and
work it until coarse crumbs form.
Mix the dough into a ball. Knead
the dough for 1–2 minutes until
smooth, then wrap in cling film
and chill in the fridge for 1–2 hours.

3 For the filling, put the sugar
and raspberries in a pan over a
low heat and gently cook for 10–12

minutes until thick. Leave to cool,
then with the back of a wooden
spoon, press half of the fruit pulp
through a sieve. Stir in the
remaining pulp.

4 Preheat the oven to 190°C
(375°F/Gas 5) and butter a tart
tin. Flour the work surface and roll
out two-thirds of the dough into a
28cm (11in) round. Use the dough
to line the tin and cut off any
excess overhanging the sides.
Spread the filling in the case.

5 Roll the rest of the dough to a
15 x 30cm (6 x 12in) rectangle.
Using a fluted wheel, for a
decorative edge (if you have one,
a sharp knife if you don't), cut the
dough into 12 x 1cm (5 x ½ in)
wide strips. Arrange half the strips
from left to right over the tart, 2cm
(¾ in) apart. Turn the tart through
45 degrees. Lay the other strips

diagonally over the top. Trim the
overhang, roll out the trimmings,
and cut 4 more strips.

6 Brush the edge of the tart with
water and fix the edge strips.
Leave to chill in the fridge for 15
minutes. Bake for 15 minutes.
Reduce the temperature to 180°C
(350°F, Gas 4) and bake for a
further 25–30 minutes. Take the
tart out of the oven, leave it to cool,
then remove from the tin. About 30
minutes before serving, lightly dust
the top with icing sugar.

Lemon meringue pie

With the sharpness of lemon combined with a smooth vanilla meringue topping, it is no wonder this pie is a family favourite..

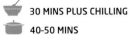

30 MINS PLUS CHILLING

40-50 MINS

SPECIAL EQUIPMENT

23cm (9in) round loose-bottomed fluted tart tin

ceramic baking beans

SERVES 8

400g (14oz) ready-made sweet shortcrust pastry

6 eggs, at room temperature, separated

3 tbsp plain flour

3 tbsp cornflour

400g (14oz) caster sugar

1 tbsp grated zest and juice of 3 lemons

45g (1½ oz) butter, diced

½ tsp cream of tartar

½ tsp vanilla extract

1 Preheat the oven to 200°C (400°F/Gas 6) and lightly butter the tin. Lightly flour a work surface and roll out the pastry. Use it to line the tin.

2 Line the pastry case with baking parchment, then fill with ceramic baking beans. Place on a baking tray and bake for 10–15 minutes, or until the pastry looks pale golden. Lift off the paper and beans, return the pastry shell to the oven, and bake for 3–5 minutes until golden. Reduce the temperature to 180°C (350°F/Gas 4). Leave to cool slightly in the tin.

3 Put the egg yolks in a bowl and lightly beat. Combine the flour, cornflour, and 225g (8oz) of the sugar in a saucepan. Slowly add 350ml (12fl oz) water and heat gently, stirring, until the sugar dissolves and there are no lumps.

Increase the heat slightly and cook, stirring, for 3–5 minutes, or until the mixture starts to thicken.

4 Beat several spoonfuls of the hot mixture into the egg yolks. Pour this mixture back into the pan and slowly bring to the boil, stirring constantly. Boil for 3 minutes, then stir in the lemon zest and juice together with the butter. Continue boiling for a further 2 minutes, or until the mixture is thick and glossy, stirring constantly and scraping down the sides of the pan as necessary. Remove the pan from the heat; cover to keep warm.

5 Whisk the egg whites in a large clean bowl until foamy. Sprinkle over the cream of tartar and whisk. Continue whisking, adding the remaining sugar, 1 tbsp at a time. Add the vanilla extract with the last tablespoon of the

sugar, whisking until the meringue is thick and glossy.

6 Place the pastry case on a baking tray, pour in the lemon filling, then top with the meringue, spreading it so it completely covers the filling right up to the pastry edge. Take care not to spill it over the pastry, or the tart will be difficult to remove from the tin after baking.

7 Place in the oven and bake for 12–15 minutes, or until the meringue is lightly golden. Transfer to a wire rack and leave to cool completely, before removing from the tin and serving.

Lemon tart

With its zesty lemon filling and buttery pastry base, this classic tart is always guaranteed to taste good.

🥣 **20 MINS PLUS CHILLING**

🍲 **55 MINS**

SPECIAL EQUIPMENT

20cm (8in) round loose-bottomed fluted tart tin

ceramic baking beans

food processor (optional)

SERVES 8

125g (4½ oz) cold butter, diced

175g (6oz) plain flour

75g (2½ oz) ground almonds

juice of 4 lemons, finely grated zest of 1 lemon

75g (2½ oz) caster sugar

3 large eggs

175ml (6fl oz) double cream

1 Preheat the oven to 200°C (400°F/Gas 6). Put the butter and flour in a mixing bowl. Using your fingertips, rub the butter into the flour until the mixture resembles breadcrumbs. Alternatively, use a food processor. Stir in the almonds, then stir in enough ice-cold water (about 3 tbsp), so the mixture comes together to form a dough. Roll the pastry out on a lightly floured work surface to a large circle about 3mm (⅛ in) thick and use to line the tart tin, pressing it into the corners. Trim away any excess around the edges, prick the bottom all over with a fork, then chill in the fridge for 30 minutes.

2 Line the pastry case with greaseproof paper and fill with ceramic baking beans. Bake in the oven for 15 minutes, then remove the paper and beans and return to the oven for a further 5 minutes, or until the pastry is cooked through. Set aside while you make the filling, and turn the oven down to 150°C (300°F/Gas 2).

3 Put the lemon juice and sugar in a mixing bowl and stir together until the sugar has dissolved. Then mix in the eggs and lemon zest. Stir in the cream and pour into the pastry case. Bake for 35 minutes, or until just set – the tart should wobble in the middle slightly when you shake the tin. Leave to cool, then chill until ready to serve. Serve with single cream.

Pear pie with walnut pastry

In this speciality from central France, wedges of pear are sandwiched between a double crust of walnut pastry. Serve the pie warm, with crème fraîche or whipped cream.

🥣 **35-40 MINS PLUS CHILLING**

🍲 **35-40 MINS**

SPECIAL EQUIPMENT

23cm (9in) round loose-bottomed fluted tart tin

SERVES 6

75g (2½ oz) walnuts, very finely chopped

500g (1lb 2oz) ready-made sweet shortcrust pastry

875g (1lb 15oz) pears

½ tsp freshly ground black pepper

juice of 1 lemon

1 tbsp caster sugar

1 Preheat the oven to 190°C (375°F/Gas 5) and brush the tart tin with melted butter. Lightly flour the work surface and knead the walnuts into the pastry. Roll out two-thirds of the dough into a 28cm (11in) round and line the tin, trimming the edges. Rewrap all excess dough and return to the fridge. Chill the pastry shell for about 1 hour, until very firm.

2 Peel, core, and quarter the pears, then put in a bowl and toss with the pepper and lemon juice. Arrange the pear wedges in a cartwheel pattern on the bottom of the pastry shell. Roll out the remaining dough into a 25cm (10in) round; stamp out a 5cm (2in) round from the centre. Place the 25cm (10in) round over the pears, trim, and press the edges together firmly to seal.

3 Brush the top of the pie with water and sprinkle with the sugar. Chill the pie for about 15 minutes until firm. Meanwhile, heat a baking sheet in the oven. Put the pie on the baking sheet so the heat starts to cook the pastry base immediately, and bake the pie for 35–40 minutes until the pastry is browned and the pears are tender when pierced with a metal skewer. If the top crust threatens to scorch before the pie is ready, cover it loosely with foil and continue to bake until the fruit is tender.

Flaky pear tartlets

These are a party favourite, a spectacular contrast of hot and cold, and need very little last-minute preparation.

🥣 **35–40 MINS PLUS CHILLING**

🍲 **30–40 MINS**

SERVES 8

450g (1lb) ready-made all-butter puff pastry

1 egg beaten with ½ tsp salt, to glaze

200g (7oz) caster sugar

120ml (4fl oz) double cream

4 pears

juice of 1 lemon

FOR THE CHANTILLY CREAM

120ml (4fl oz) double cream

1–2 tsp icing sugar

½ tsp vanilla extract)

1 Sprinkle 2 baking sheets with cold water. Roll out the puff pastry dough, cut in half lengthways, then cut diagonally at 10cm (4in) intervals along the length of each piece, to make 8 diamond shapes. Transfer to the baking sheets and brush with the glaze. With the tip of a knife, score a border around each. Chill for 15 minutes.

2 Preheat the oven to 220°C (425°F/Gas 7). Bake the cases for about 15 minutes, until they start to brown, then reduce the temperature to 190°C (375°F/Gas 5) and bake for 20–25 minutes more, until golden and crisp. Transfer to wire racks to cool, then cut out the lid from each case and scoop out any under-cooked pastry from inside.

3 Put 120ml (4fl oz) water in a saucepan and dissolve 150g (5½oz) of the sugar. Boil, without stirring, until golden. Reduce the heat. Remove from the heat, stand back, and add the cream. Heat gently until the caramel dissolves. Cool.

4 Whip the cream for the Chantilly cream until soft peaks form. Add the icing sugar and vanilla, and continue whipping until stiff peaks form. Chill.

5 Butter a baking sheet. Heat the grill. Peel and core the pears. Thinly slice lengthways, keeping attached at the stalk end. Flatten with your fingers, transfer to the sheet, brush with lemon, and sprinkle with the remaining sugar. Grill until caramelized.

6 Transfer the pastry cases to plates and place Chantilly cream and a pear fan in each. Pour a little cold caramel sauce over each fan and partially cover with the pastry lids.

Tarte tatin

The special deliciousness of this upside-down tart comes from cooking the apples in the caramel itself.

🥣 **45–50 MINS PLUS CHILLING**

🍲 **20–25 MINS**

SERVES 8

14–16 apples, about 2.4kg (5lb 6oz)

1 lemon, halved

125g (4½ oz) unsalted butter

200g (7oz) caster sugar

250g (9oz) ready-made sweet shortcrust pastry

crème fraîche, to serve

1 With a vegetable peeler, carefully peel the apples, then halve and core them. Rub the apples all over with the cut lemon to prevent discoloration.

2 Melt the butter in a heavy, ovenproof frying pan. Add the sugar. Cook over a medium heat, stirring occasionally, for 3–5 minutes, until caramelized to a deep golden brown. Remove from the heat and allow to cool to tepid. Arrange the apple halves over in concentric circles to fill the pan, packing them tightly.

3 Cook the apples over a high heat for 15–25 minutes, until caramelized. Turn once to caramelize on both sides. Remove from the heat and leave to cool for 10–15 minutes.

4 Meanwhile, preheat the oven to 190°C (375°F/Gas 5). Roll out the pastry to a circle about 2.5cm (1in) larger than the pan. Roll up the dough around the rolling pin, then drape it over the pan. Tuck the edges around the apples. Bake for 20–25 minutes, until golden brown. Let cool, then set a plate on top, hold firmly together, and invert. If any apples stick to the pan, replace on the tart. Spoon some caramel over the apples. Serve with crème fraîche.

Peach and nectarine puff pastry tart

If you don't have time to make puff pastry at home, ready-made versions are just as good. You can buy it in a block or ready-rolled, as suggested for this recipe.

🥣 **20 MINS PLUS CHILLING**

🍲 **20 MINS**

❄️ **FREEZABLE**

SPECIAL EQUIPMENT

electric hand whisk

SERVES 8

1 large egg, plus 1 large egg yolk

50g (1¾ oz) golden caster sugar

25g (scant 1oz) plain flour

300ml (10fl oz) milk

juice of 1 lemon

375g packet ready-rolled puff pastry

1 egg yolk, beaten, to glaze

4 ripe peaches, halved and stoned

4 ripe nectarines, halved and stoned

icing sugar, for dusting

1 Put the egg, egg yolk, sugar, and flour in a mixing bowl and whisk with an electric hand whisk until well combined. Heat the milk in a pan until almost boiling, then slowly whisk into the egg mixture with the lemon juice. Return the mixture to the pan and slowly bring to the boil, stirring continuously.

Cook for a couple of minutes, then transfer to a bowl. Sit a piece of greaseproof paper on the surface so the custard doesn't form a skin, then leave to cool.

2 Meanwhile, on a lightly floured work surface, roll the pastry out into a 23 x 30cm (9 x 12in) rectangle and place on a lightly oiled baking sheet. With a knife, score a rectangle on it, leaving a 2cm (¾in) border all round the edge. Press the back of the knife into the border to make horizontal lines – these will ensure the pastry rises. Prick the base of the rectangle with a fork and place in the fridge for 20 minutes. Preheat the oven to 200°C (400°F/Gas 6).

3 Once the pastry has chilled, brush the border with the beaten egg yolk, then bake for 20 minutes, or until the pastry is cooked and golden. Push the inner rectangle down slightly, then leave to cool for 30 minutes.

4 Spoon in the custard, then top with the fruit, dust with icing sugar, and serve.

Peach pie

Less famous than its cherry cousin but no less tasty, this American classic with a latticed top is a splendid summer dessert. Choose perfectly ripe peaches full of juice.

🥣 **40-45 MINS PLUS CHILLING**

🍲 **40-45 MINS**

SPECIAL EQUIPMENT

23cm (9in) pie dish

SERVES 8

280g (9½ oz) plain flour

salt

125g (4½ oz) lard or white vegetable fat, chilled

75g (2½ oz) unsalted butter, chilled

4-5 ripe peaches

150g (5½ oz) granulated sugar

1-2 tbsp lemon juice, to taste

1 egg

1 Sift 250g (9oz) of the flour and ½ tsp salt into a bowl. Dice the lard and butter, and rub into the flour with your fingers until crumbs form. Sprinkle with 3 tbsp water and mix until the dough turns into a ball. Wrap in cling film and chill for 30 minutes.

2 Preheat the oven to 200°C (400°F/Gas 6) and put in a baking sheet. On a floured surface, roll out two-thirds of the dough and use to line the dish with some overhang. Press the dough into the dish and chill for 15 minutes.

3 Immerse the peaches in boiling water for 10 seconds, then plunge into iced water. Halve the peaches, remove the stones, and peel off the skins. Cut into 1cm (½ in) slices and put in a large bowl. Sprinkle with the remaining flour, sugar, salt, and lemon juice. Stir, then transfer to the pastry case with their juices.

4 Roll out the remaining dough into a rectangle. Cut out 8 strips, each 1cm (½ in) wide, and arrange them in a lattice-like pattern on top of the pie; trim the pastry. Beat the egg with ½ tsp salt and use this to glaze the lattice and secure the strips to the edge of the pie. Bake for 40–45 minutes until the pastry is golden brown. Serve at room temperature or chilled, with a dollop of cream.

Bavarian plum tart

Bavaria is famous for its cakes and tarts. In this recipe, a quick version of brioche forms the base. Juice from the fruit mingles with the custard filling to bring about a deliciously moist result. Apricots are also delicious in this tart.

 **35–40 MINS PLUS RISING AND STANDING**

50–55 MINS

SPECIAL EQUIPMENT

28cm (11in) round quiche dish

SERVES 8–10

1½ tsp dried yeast, or 9g (⅓oz) fresh yeast

375g (13oz) plain flour, more if needed

2 tbsp caster sugar

1 tsp salt

3 eggs

125g (4½ oz) unsalted butter, softened

FOR THE FILLING

2 tbsp dried breadcrumbs

875g (1lb 15oz) purple plums, stoned and quartered

2 egg yolks

60ml (2fl oz) double cream

100g (3½ oz) caster sugar

1 Sprinkle or crumble the yeast over 60ml (2fl oz) lukewarm water in a small bowl. Let stand for 5 minutes, until dissolved. Lightly oil a medium bowl. Sift the flour onto a work surface, make a well in the centre, and add the sugar, salt, yeast mixture, and eggs.

2 With your fingertips, work the ingredients in the well until they are thoroughly mixed. Work in the flour to form a soft dough; adding more flour if it is very sticky. Knead on a floured work surface for 10 minutes, until very elastic. Work in more flour as needed, so that the dough is slightly sticky, but peels easily from the work surface.

3 Add the butter to the dough, pinch and squeeze to mix it in, then knead until smooth. Shape into a ball and put it into the oiled bowl. Cover, and let rise in the fridge for 1½–2 hours, until doubled in size.

4 Brush the quiche dish with melted butter. Knead the dough lightly to knock out the air. Flour a work surface; roll out the dough into a 32cm (13in) round. Wrap it around the rolling pin and drape it over the dish. Press it into the bottom and up the side of the dish. Trim off the excess and sprinkle the breadcrumbs over the bottom. Preheat the oven to 220°C (425°F/Gas 7). Put a baking sheet in the oven to heat.

5 Arrange the plum wedges, cut-side up, in circles on the brioche shell. Let stand at room temperature for 30–45 minutes, until the edge of the dough is puffed. Put the egg yolks, double cream, and two-thirds of the sugar into a bowl. Whisk together. Sprinkle the plum wedges with the remaining sugar and bake the tart on the baking sheet for 5 minutes. Reduce the heat to 180°C (350°F/Gas 4).

6 Ladle the custard mixture over the fruit, return the tart to the oven, and continue baking for 45–50 minutes longer, until the dough is browned, the fruit is tender, and the custard is set. Let the tart cool on a wire rack. Serve warm or at room temperature.

Hazelnut, chocolate, and orange tart

With a base made of pasta frolla, an Italian sweet pastry, this is a most delicious recipe for a special occasion. The tart contains a richly flavoured filling of ground hazelnuts, plain chocolate, and orange zest, all topped with a chocolate glaze.

45–50 MINS PLUS CHILLING

35–40 MINS

SPECIAL EQUIPMENT

23cm (9in) round fluted springform tin

food processor

SERVES 6–8

FOR THE PASTA FROLLA DOUGH

150g (5½ oz) plain flour, plus more if needed

75g (2½ oz) unsalted butter, softened

50g (1¾ oz) caster sugar

¼ tsp salt

grated zest of 1 orange

1 egg

FOR THE FILLING

pared zest of 2 oranges

125g (4½oz) hazelnuts

100g (3½ oz) caster sugar

150g (5½ oz) unsalted butter

2 tsp plain flour

2 egg yolks, plus 1 egg

60g (2oz) plain chocolate, grated

FOR THE CHOCOLATE GLAZE

125g (4½ oz) plain chocolate

75g (2½ oz) unsalted butter, diced

2 tsp Grand Marnier

1 For the dough, sift the flour onto a work surface and make a well in the centre. Put the rest of the ingredients into the well and work with your fingertips until thoroughly mixed. Work in the flour until coarse crumbs form, then press into a ball. If it is sticky, work in a little more flour. Lightly flour the work surface and knead the dough for 1–2 minutes until very smooth. Shape into a ball, wrap tightly, and chill for about 30 minutes until firm.

2 Brush the tin with melted butter. Lightly flour a work surface, roll the dough into a 28cm (11in) round and use it to line the tin, pressing it into the corners. Trim away the excess. With your thumbs, press the dough evenly up the sides of the tin to increase the height of the rim. Prick the bottom all over with a fork, then chill for 15 minutes until firm.

3 Meanwhile, bring a pan of water to the boil, add the pared orange zest, and simmer for 2 minutes. Drain, rinse with cold water, drain again, and coarsely chop two-thirds of it.

4 Preheat the oven to 180°C (350°F/Gas 4). For the filling, spread the nuts on a baking sheet and toast in the oven for 6–15 minutes (watch them closely) until lightly browned. Rub in a tea towel to remove the skins and set aside to cool. Leave the oven on.

5 Once cool, blitz the nuts with the sugar in a food processor. Beat the butter in a mixing bowl until creamy. Add the flour and nut mix and beat until light and fluffy. Add the yolks and egg, one at a time, beating after each addition. Mix in the chocolate and chopped orange zest, then spread the filling over the pastry shell. Bake on a baking sheet for 35–40 minutes, or until a knife inserted in the centre comes out clean. Allow to cool on a wire rack.

6 For the glaze, break the chocolate into chunks and heat in a bowl set over a pan of hot water (the base of the bowl must not touch the water) until melted. Gently stir the butter into the chocolate in 2–3 batches. Add the Grand Marnier, then let cool to tepid. Unmould the tart and spread the glaze over the top. Slice the remaining cooked orange zest into fine julienne strips and use to decorate the top.

Auvergne torte

This warming pie from France is an ideal lunch when it's cold outside; it's very comforting in the depths of winter..

🥣 **30 MINS, PLUS CHILLING**

🍲 **1 HR 15 MINS**

❄️ **FREEZABLE**

SPECIAL EQUIPMENT

23cm (9in) deep-dish metal pie tin with sloping sides

SERVES 8

FOR THE FILLING

30g (1oz) butter

1 large onion, finely sliced

1 garlic clove, finely chopped

100g (3½ oz) bacon lardons

650g (1lb 6oz) waxy new potatoes, peeled and finely sliced

100g (3½ oz) Cantal cheese, or Wensleydale or mild Cheddar, grated

1 tbsp finely chopped flat-leaf parsley

salt and freshly ground black pepper

200ml (7fl oz) single cream

1 egg yolk

FOR THE PASTRY

500g (1lb 2oz) ready-made puff pastry

plain flour, for dusting

1 egg yolk, beaten with 1 tbsp cold water, to glaze

1 Melt the butter in a large saucepan. Add the onion and cook over a medium heat for 10 minutes. Add the garlic and bacon and cook for a further 5 minutes until the onion is soft, but not brown.

2 Preheat the oven to 180°C (350°F/Gas 4). Roll out the puff pastry on a floured surface and, using a 23cm (9in) deep-dish metal pie tin as a template, cut from one end a circle large enough to top the pie. Use the rest of the pastry to line the tin, leaving a 1cm (½ in) overhang around the edges. Wrap and chill the base and the top for 20 minutes.

3 Brush the inside of the pastry case, including the edges, with some of the egg yolk mixture. Reserve the remainder.

4 Layer the pastry case with one-third of the potatoes. Cover them with half the onion and bacon mixture and half the cheese. Scatter over half the parsley and season with salt and pepper.

5 Repeat the procedure and finish with a final layer of potatoes. Whisk together the cream and the egg yolk, and pour it over the pie filling. Top the pie with the pre-cut circle of pastry, pressing it down around the edges to seal. Crimp the edges.

6 Brush the top of the pie with the remaining egg yolk mixture and cut 2 small slits in the top to allow steam to escape. Place the pie on a baking tray and bake for 1 hour until well cooked, puffed up, and golden brown. Set aside to rest for 15–20 minutes before serving.

Bread
and pizza

Mini pizzas

These individual pizzas are perfect party-sized children's snacks, and can be topped and cooked at the last minute.

🥣 **20 MINS, PLUS RISING**

🍲 **10 MINS**

SPECIAL EQUIPMENT

food processor with dough hook (optional)

MAKES 10

FOR THE BASES

250g (9oz) strong bread flour, plus extra for dusting

¼ tsp salt

1½ tsp dried yeast

1 tbsp olive oil, plus extra for greasing

FOR THE TOPPING

400g can crushed tomatoes, or 400ml (14fl oz) passata

2 garlic cloves, crushed

1 tbsp olive oil

freshly ground black pepper

selection of prepared pizza toppings

150g (5½ oz) finely sliced mozzarella

1 Put the flour and salt into a large bowl, or the bowl of a food processor fitted with a dough hook. Dissolve the yeast in 175ml (6fl oz) of warm water, then add the oil.

2 If making by hand, make a well in the centre of the flour. Gradually pour in the liquid, stirring to form a rough dough. Use your hands to bring it together. Turn the dough out onto a floured work surface. Knead for up to 10 minutes, until smooth, glossy, and elastic.

3 If making in a food processor, turn the machine on to a low speed. Pour in the liquid a little at a time, until the mixture begins to come together. You may need to turn off the machine and scrape down the sides once or twice to ensure that all the flour is incorporated. Increase the speed to medium and continue to knead for 5–7 minutes, until smooth, glossy, and elastic.

4 Put the dough in an oiled bowl and cover loosely with cling film. Leave to rise in a warm place for 2 hours, or until doubled in size.

5 Meanwhile, make the tomato sauce. Put the tomatoes, garlic, and olive oil into a small saucepan, and season well with pepper. Bring to the boil, reduce the heat to a low simmer, and cook for 45 minutes to 1 hour, until you have a rich, thick sauce. Adjust the seasoning.

6 When ready to cook, preheat the oven to 230°C (450°F/Gas 8). When the dough has risen, turn it out onto a lightly floured work surface and knead it briefly. Divide it into 10 equal-sized pieces, and roll each one out to a diameter of 12–15cm (5–6in). Lay them on several baking sheets.

7 Top the mini pizzas with tbsp of the tomato sauce, spread thinly, and any toppings you would like. Finish with a thin layer of mozzarella cheese, and cook at the top of the hot oven for 10 minutes, until golden brown and crispy.

Pizza bianca with four cheeses

Literally meaning "white pizza", this cheesy dish is traditionally made without tomato sauce.
You could sprinkle with pine nuts and raisins before it goes in the oven.

10 MINS, PLUS RISING

10-15 MINS

MAKES 1

olive oil, for greasing

1 ball basic pizza dough

plain flour, for dusting

semolina, for sprinkling

FOR THE TOPPING

75g (2½ oz) mozzarella,
  torn into pieces

handful of freshly grated
  Parmesan cheese

25g (scant 1oz) Gorgonzola or
  other blue cheese, crumbled

25g (scant 1oz) Gruyère
  cheese, grated

pinch of dried oregano

1 Preheat the oven to 240°C (475°F/Gas 9). Very lightly grease a baking tray and place it in the oven to heat.

2 Place the dough on a floured surface and use a rolling pin to roll it out as thin as you can – about 25–30cm (10–12in) in diameter. Sprinkle the hot baking tray with semolina and transfer the dough onto it. Remember to wear an oven mitt before transferring the dough, as the baking tray will be hot. Set the tray on a heat-resistant surface, like a wooden cutting board. Then, quickly lower the dough onto the center of the tray, leaving at least an inch and a half of free space around the rim, so it's easier to work with.

3 Cover each quarter segment of the pizza with a different cheese, using the 4 cheeses or more of the one you prefer. Sprinkle over the oregano, then bake for 10–15 minutes or until the crust and base are crispy and the cheese is lightly golden and melted.

Four seasons pizza

A visual treat, this single dish makes you feel like you are eating
four different types of pizza. Feel free to vary the toppings.

🥣 **20 MINS**

🍲 **COOK 35–40 MINS**

MAKES 1

1 tbsp unsalted butter

1 shallot, finely chopped

¼ tbsp olive oil, plus extra
for greasing

1 bay leaf

1 garlic clove, crushed

250g (9oz) ripe plum tomatoes,
deseeded and chopped

¼ tbsp tomato purée

¼ tbsp caster sugar

sea salt and freshly ground pepper

1 basic pizza base

plain flour, for dusting

FOR THE TOPPING

45g (1½ oz) mozzarella, thinly sliced

30g (1oz) mushrooms, thinly sliced

¼ tbsp extra virgin olive oil

1 roasted red pepper, thinly sliced

2 anchovy fillets, halved lengthways

30g (1oz) pepperoni, thinly sliced

½ tbsp capers

2 artichoke hearts, halved

handful of black olives

1 For the sauce, place a pan over
a low heat. Add the butter,
shallot, oil, bay leaf, and garlic. Stir,
cover, and sweat the ingredients
together for 5–6 minutes, stirring
occasionally. Add the tomatoes,
tomato purée, and sugar. Cook for
5 minutes, stirring. Pour in 60ml
(2fl oz) water, bring to the boil, and
reduce the heat to a simmer. Cook
for 15 minutes, stirring, until
reduced to a thick sauce. Season to
taste. Using a wooden spoon, press
the sauce through a sieve. Cover
and chill until needed.

2 Preheat the oven to 200°C
(400°F/Gas 6). Grease a baking
tray and place the pizza base onto
the tray. Spread the sauce over the
base, leaving a 2cm (¾ in) border
around the edge. Place any leftover
sauce in a small freezerproof
container and freeze for later use.

3 Top the pizza with mozzarella
and arrange the mushroom
slices on a quarter of the pizza and
brush with extra virgin olive oil.
Pile the roasted pepper slices on
another quarter with the anchovy
fillets on top. Use pepperoni and
capers for the third and artichokes
and olives for the fourth quarter.
Bake in the top shelf of the oven,
for 15 minutes or until golden
brown. Serve hot.

Pizza Florentina

An eye-catching pizza topped with spinach and a whole egg.
This is a wonderful way to get the children to eat greens.

🥣 **10 MINS, PLUS RISING**

🍲 **20 MINS**

MAKES 1

olive oil, for greasing

1 ball basic pizza dough

plain flour, for dusting

FOR THE TOPPING

150g (5½ oz) tomato pasta sauce

75g (2½ oz) spinach, cooked and chopped

¼ tsp freshly grated nutmeg

½ tsp thyme leaves

50g (1¾ oz) mozzarella cheese, sliced

1 egg

1 tbsp grated Parmesan cheese

freshly ground black pepper

1 Preheat the oven to 200°C (400°F/Gas 6). Very lightly grease a baking tray and place it in the oven to heat.

2 Place the dough on a floured surface and use a rolling pin to roll it out into a 23cm (9in) round. Lift the round onto a greased baking tray and spread with tomato sauce, leaving a 2.5cm (1in) border.

3 Spread spinach on top, in an even layer, and sprinkle with nutmeg and thyme. Lay on the cheese slices and crack an egg over. Sprinkle with Parmesan. Bake for 20 minutes or until the dough edges are crisp. Season to taste with black pepper and serve.

Pizza with spinach and ricotta cheese

It is important to squeeze excess liquid from the spinach to prevent the pizza base from becoming soggy.

 15 MINS PLUS RISING

10 MINS

MAKES 1

125g (4½ oz) strong white flour

pinch of salt

pinch of caster sugar

¾ tsp easy-blend dried yeast

1 tbsp olive oil

90ml (3fl oz) warm water

a little semolina, for sprinkling

2–3 tbsp passata

200g (7oz) spinach leaves, wilted and drained

2–3 tbsp ricotta cheese

1 Sift the flour, salt, and sugar into a bowl. Add the yeast. Stir in the oil and enough warm water to form a soft but not sticky dough.

2 Place the dough on a slightly floured surface, and knead gently for several minutes until smooth and elastic. Return to the bowl, cover with oiled cling film, and place for about 40 minutes, until the dough has doubled in size.

3 Preheat the oven to its highest setting. Place a lightly oiled baking tray in the oven to get hot. Turn out the dough onto a floured surface and briefly re-knead to knock out the air (called knocking back). Roll out thinly into a round, about 25cm (10in) diameter. Sprinkle the hot baking tray with semolina and transfer the pizza base onto it, spreading it out firmly again.

4 Spoon and smooth the passata onto the pizza base, using the back of the spoon. Squeeze any liquid from the spinach, then spread it on the passata. Dot with spoonfuls of ricotta cheese, season with black pepper, and bake for 10 minutes, or until the crust and base are golden and crispy.

Pizza with tomatoes, olives, and capers

This thin-based Italian-style pizza is ideal for using up a glut of homegrown summer tomatoes.

10 MINS PLUS RISING

15 MINS

❄ FREEZABLE

MAKES 1

2–3 tbsp passata

3 tomatoes, sliced

handful of pitted black olives

1–2 tsp capers, rinsed

pinch of freshly ground black pepper

FOR THE PIZZA DOUGH

125g (4½ oz) strong white flour

pinch of salt

pinch of caster sugar

¾ tsp easy-blend dried yeast

1 tbsp olive oil

a little semolina, for sprinkling

1 Sift the flour, salt, and sugar into a bowl. Add the yeast. Stir in the oil and enough warm water to form a soft but not sticky dough (about 90ml/3fl oz).

2 Place the dough on a slightly floured surface and knead gently for several minutes until smooth and elastic. Return to the bowl, cover with oiled cling film, and leave in a warm place for about 40 minutes, until the dough has doubled in size.

3 Preheat the oven to its highest setting. Very lightly oil a baking tray and put it in the oven to get hot. The baking tray and the oil both need to be really hot before cooking the pizza.

4 Place the dough on a floured surface and roll it out as thinly as you can; about 25–30cm (10–12in) in diameter. Sprinkle the hot baking tray with a little semolina and transfer the pizza dough onto it.

5 Spoon the passata onto the pizza base, using the back of the spoon to smooth it out evenly. Top with the tomato slices, then arrange the olives and capers on top. Bake for 10–15 minutes, or until the crust and base are crisp and golden. Season with black pepper and serve.

Three-pepper pizza with cheese

Choose brightly coloured, firm peppers with no soft spots,
and add finely sliced chillies instead of cayenne, if you prefer.

🥘 1 HR 15 MINS PLUS STANDING

🍲 20-25 MINS

SERVES 4-6

125g (4½ oz) strong plain flour

salt and freshly ground black pepper

pinch of sugar

¾ tsp easy-blend dried yeast

5 tbsp olive oil

2 onions, thinly sliced

2 red peppers, deseeded and cut into strips

1 green pepper, deseeded and cut into strips

1 yellow pepper, deseeded and cut into strips

3 garlic cloves, finely chopped

small bunch of any herb, such as rosemary, thyme, basil, or parsley, or a mixture, leaves finely chopped

cayenne, to taste

175g (6oz) mozzarella cheese, sliced

1 Sift the flour, a pinch of salt, and the sugar into a bowl and add the yeast. Stir in 1 tbsp of the oil and add up to 90ml (3fl oz) warm water to form a soft, but not sticky, dough. Knead gently on a floured work surface for several minutes until smooth and elastic. Return to the bowl, cover with oiled cling film, and leave in a warm place (you can preheat the oven and leave the bowl on top of the hob above) for 30–40 minutes, or until doubled in size.

2 Heat 1 tbsp of the oil in a frying pan, add the onions, and stir for 2–3 minutes until soft. Transfer to a bowl and set aside. Add the remaining oil to the pan, then add the peppers, garlic, and half the herbs. Season with salt and cayenne. Sauté, stirring, for 7–10 minutes until soft. Taste for seasoning; it should be quite spicy.

3 Preheat the oven to 230°C (450°F/Gas 8). Put a baking sheet near the bottom of the oven to heat up and generously flour a second baking sheet. Turn the dough out onto a floured work surface again and knock it back by re-kneading briefly. Roll out the dough thinly to a round, about 25cm (10in) in diameter. Transfer the pizza base to the floured baking sheet and press up the edge to form a shallow rim, if you like.

4 Spread the onions and then the peppers, evenly over the pizza base, leaving a 2cm (¾ in) border all around the edge (if you haven't made a shallow rim), so it can become golden in the oven.

Spoon any remaining oil from the frying pan over the peppers and top them evenly with the slices of mozzarella. Let the assembled pizza stand in a warm place for 10–15 minutes, until the dough has puffed up well around the edges. Don't leave it for any longer, as it should be baked as soon as possible to retain maximum flavour.

5 With a sharp, jerking movement, slide the pizza onto the heated baking sheet at the bottom of the oven. Bake for about 20–25 minutes, or until brown all over and the cheese has melted. If you are using finely sliced chilli instead of cayenne, add it 5 minutes before the end of the cooking time. Remove from the oven, scatter the reserved herbs over the top of the pizza, and serve.

Pizza bianca with Parma ham, rocket, and mozzarella

You can cut the Parma ham into pieces with a pair of scissors, so that the pizza is easier to eat.

 **10 MINS, PLUS RISING**

10 MINS

MAKES 1

olive oil, for greasing

1 ball basic pizza dough

plain flour, for dusting

semolina, for sprinkling

FOR THE TOPPING

200g (7oz) mozzarella,
    torn into chunks

freshly ground black pepper

4 slices Parma ham

handful of wild rocket

1 Preheat the oven to 240°C (475°F/Gas 9). Very lightly grease a baking tray and place it in the oven to heat.

2 Place the dough on a floured surface and use a rolling pin to roll it out as thin as you can – about 25–30cm (10–12in) in diameter. Sprinkle the hot baking tray with semolina and transfer the dough onto it. Remember to wear an oven mitt before transferring the dough, as the baking tray will be hot. Set the tray on a heat-resistant surface, like a wooden cutting board. Then, quickly lower the dough onto the center of the tray, leaving at least an inch and a half of free space around the rim, so it's easier to work with.

3 Top the base with the mozzarella, season with lots of black pepper, then bake for 10 minutes or until the crust and base are crispy, and the top is melted. Drape the Parma ham on top, scatter evenly with the rocket, season again with black pepper, and serve.

Onion confit and gorgonzola pizzas

Onions and Gorgonzola are delicious together, topping a crust made crunchy with fine yellow cornmeal or polenta.

40–45 MINS PLUS RISING

35–40 MINS

MAKES 6

250g (9oz) unbleached strong white flour, plus more if needed

1½ tsp fast-action yeast

2 tbsp olive oil

75g (2½ oz) fine yellow cornmeal or polenta

175g (6oz) Gorgonzola cheese, cut into slices

FOR THE ONION CONFIT

2 tbsp olive oil

750g (1lb 10oz) red onions, thinly sliced

2 tsp sugar

salt and freshly ground black pepper

4 tbsp red wine

5–7 sprigs of oregano, leaves picked and chopped, plus reserve some to serve

1 Sift the flour into a bowl and add the yeast. Stir in the oil and enough warm water (about 150ml/5fl oz) to form a soft, but not sticky, dough. Knead gently on a lightly floured surface for several minutes until smooth and elastic. Return to the bowl, cover with oiled cling film, and leave to rise in a warm place for about 40 minutes until the dough has doubled in size.

2 For the onion confit, heat the oil in a frying pan over a medium heat. Add the onions and sugar, and season with salt and pepper. Cook for 5–7 minutes, stirring often, until the onions are soft and lightly brown. Add the wine and continue cooking until it has evaporated. Reduce the heat, press a piece of foil on top of the onions, and cover with a lid. Cook, stirring occasionally, for 15–20 minutes, or until the onions are soft enough to cut with a spoon. Let cool. Stir in the chopped oregano leaves.

3 Preheat the oven to 230°C (450°F/Gas 8). Put 2 baking sheets on separate racks in the bottom half of the oven to heat. Cut 6 x 23cm (9in) squares of foil and sprinkle each generously with the cornmeal or polenta.

4 Turn out the dough onto a floured surface and knock it back by re-kneading briefly. With your hands, roll the dough into a cylinder about 5cm (2in) in diameter. Cut the cylinder in half, then cut each half into 3 equal pieces. Shape the pieces of dough into balls.

5 Roll out a ball of dough into an 18cm (7in) round. Transfer the round to 1 of the squares of foil. Repeat to shape the remaining dough. If you like, press up the edges of the rounds with your fingertips to form shallow rims. Spread the rounds with the onion confit.

6 Top the rounds with slices of the cheese and leave them in a warm place for about 15 minutes, until the dough is puffed. Bake the pizzas, on the foil, on the baking sheets, for 15–20 minutes until lightly browned and crisp. Switch the baking sheets after 7 minutes so the pizzas brown evenly. Serve the pizzas hot from the oven. Brush the crusts with oil and top them with the reserved oregano leaves.

Chicago deep-dish pizza

A hearty pizza dating back to 1940s Chicago. The dough can be made, kneaded, and left to rise in the refrigerator overnight, if it's more convenient.

35–40 MINS, PLUS RISING

20–25 MINS

SPECIAL EQUIPMENT

35cm (14in) pizza pan, or
2 x 23cm (9in) cake tins

MAKES 1 LARGE
OR 2 SMALL

2½ tsp fast-action dried yeast,
or 15g (½ oz) fresh yeast

500g (1lb 2oz) unbleached strong
white flour, plus more if needed

2 tsp salt

3 tbsp olive oil, plus extra
for greasing

2–3 tbsp polenta (fine
yellow cornmeal)

FOR THE TOPPING

375g (13oz) mild Italian sausage

1 tbsp olive oil

3 garlic cloves, finely chopped

2 x 400g cans chopped
plum tomatoes

freshly ground black pepper

leaves from 7–10 flat-leaf parsley
sprigs, chopped

175g (6oz) mozzarella cheese,
chopped or torn into small chunks

1 In a small bowl, crumble the yeast over 4 tablespoons of lukewarm water. Let stand for 5 minutes until dissolved, stirring once. Place the flour onto a work surface with the salt. Make a well in the centre and add the yeast, 300ml (10fl oz) of lukewarm water, and the oil. With your fingertips, work the liquid ingredients in the centre of the well until mixed. Draw in the flour and work it into the other ingredients to form a smooth dough; it should be soft and slightly sticky.

2 Dust the dough and your hands with flour, and begin to knead by holding the dough with one hand, and pushing it away from you with the other. Peel the dough from the surface, give it a quarter turn, and knead for 5–7 minutes until smooth, elastic, and it forms a ball. If the dough sticks, flour the work surface. Place the dough in an oiled bowl and flip it so the surface is lightly oiled. Cover with a damp, clean tea towel and let rise in a warm place for 1–1½ hours until doubled in size.

3 Slit the side of each sausage and push out the meat, discarding the casing. Heat the oil in a pan and fry the sausage meat over a medium-high heat, breaking it up with a wooden spoon, for 5–7 minutes until cooked. Reduce the heat to medium, remove the meat from the pan, and pour off all but 1 tablespoon of the fat. Stir the garlic into the pan and fry for 30 seconds. Return the sausage and stir in the tomatoes, salt, black pepper, and all but 1 tablespoon of the parsley. Cook, stirring, for 10–15 minutes until the sauce has thickened.

Remove from the heat, taste for seasoning, and let cool.

4 Brush the pizza pan, or cake tins, with oil and sprinkle the polenta in the pan, or tins, and turn it to coat the bottom and side, then turn upside down and remove the excess. Turn the dough onto a lightly floured work surface and knock out the air for 15–20 seconds. Cover and rest for 5 minutes.

5 Shape the dough into a loose ball and roll into a round, or rounds. Wrap around the rolling pin and drape over the pan or tins. Press into the bottom of the pan or tins, and 2.5cm (1in) up the side. Cover with a dry, clean tea towel and let rise for 20 minutes. Preheat the oven to 230°C (450°F/Gas 8) and place in a baking tray to heat. Spread the sauce over the dough, leaving a border. Sprinkle over the cheese and the remaining parsley. Bake for 20–25 minutes until crisp and golden.

Beetroot, courgette, and goat's cheese pizzas

For a colourful variation, use red or yellow peppers instead of courgettes, and slices of baby Camembert in place of goat's cheese.

30 MINS, PLUS RISING

20 MINS

MAKES 2 LARGE OR 4 SMALL

5 tbsp olive oil

4 small courgettes, sliced

1 red onion, halved and thinly sliced

1 large garlic clove, finely chopped

2 tbsp chopped rosemary

1 ball basic pizza dough

150ml (5fl oz) passata

2 tbsp tomato purée

2 cooked beetroots (in natural juices), diced

4 handfuls of wild rocket, plus extra to garnish

2 x 120g cylinders goat's cheese, sliced

coarse sea salt

freshly ground black pepper

1 Heat 3 tablespoons of oil in a frying pan. Add the courgettes, onion, garlic, and rosemary and cook, stirring, for 3 minutes until softened, but not browned. Set aside.

2 Preheat the oven to 220°C (425°F/Gas 7). Knead the dough and roll out to two 30–35cm (12–14in) rounds or four 20cm (8in) rounds and place on oiled pizza plates or baking trays. Press out the rounds again with floured fingers, then place in the oven and bake for 10 minutes to cook them partially.

3 Mix the passata with the tomato purée. Remove the pizzas from the oven and spread the tomato mixture over, followed by the courgette and onion mixture. Scatter with the beetroot and rocket, then arrange the goat's cheese slices on top. Sprinkle each with a little salt and pepper.

4 Bake in the oven for a further 10 minutes until the crust is golden brown, the cheese is melting, and everything is hot through. Top with a little rocket and drizzle each pizza with the remaining oil before serving.

Pissaladière

This French version of the Italian pizza derives its name from pissala, a paste made from anchovies.

🥣 **20 MINS, PLUS RISING**

🍲 **1 HOUR 20 MINS**

❄️ **FREEZABLE**

SPECIAL EQUIPMENT

32.5 x 23cm (13 x 9in) Swiss roll tin

SERVES 4

225g (8oz) strong white bread flour, plus extra for dusting

sea salt and freshly ground black pepper

1 tsp soft brown sugar

1 tsp dried yeast

1 tbsp olive oil, plus extra for greasing

FOR THE TOPPING

4 tbsp olive oil

900g (2lb) onions, finely sliced

3 garlic cloves

sprig of thyme

1 tsp herbes de Provence (dry mix of thyme, basil, rosemary, and oregano)

1 bay leaf

100g jar anchovies in oil

12 pitted black niçoise olives, or Italian olives

1 For the base, mix the flour, 1 teaspoon salt, and black pepper to taste in a large bowl. Pour 150ml (5fl oz) lukewarm water into a separate bowl, and use a fork to whisk in the sugar, then the yeast. Set aside for 10 minutes to froth, then pour into the flour with the olive oil.

2 Mix together to form a dough, adding 1–2 tablespoons of lukewarm water if it looks too dry. Turn the dough out onto a lightly floured surface and knead for 10 minutes or until smooth and elastic. Shape it into a ball, place in a lightly oiled bowl, and cover with a clean tea towel. Leave in a warm place for 1 hour or until doubled in size.

3 For the topping, pour the oil in a saucepan over a very low heat. Add the onions, garlic, herbs, and bay leaf. Cover and sweat gently, stirring occasionally, for 1 hour or until the onions look like a purée. Be careful not to let the onions catch; if they begin to stick, add a little water. Drain well and set aside, discarding the bay leaf.

4 Preheat the oven to 180°C (350°F/Gas 4). Knead the dough briefly on a lightly floured surface, and roll it out so it is thin and large enough to fit in the tin. Press the dough into the tin and prick it with a fork.

5 Spread the onions over the base. Drain the anchovies, reserving 3 tablespoons oil, and slice the fillets in half lengthways. Embed the olives in rows in the dough and drape the fillets in a criss-cross pattern on top of the onions. Drizzle with the reserved anchovy oil and sprinkle with black pepper.

6 Bake for 25 minutes or until the crust is brown. The onions should not brown or dry out. Remove and serve warm, cut into rectangles, squares, or wedges, or allow to cool before serving.

Calzone with cheese, ham, and spinach

Calzone is a folded Italian pizza. For a crispy finish, sprinkle the top of the dough with some water before baking.

🍴 15 MINS

🍲 20 MINS

MAKES 1

FOR THE DOUGH

125g (4½ oz) strong plain flour

pinch of salt

pinch of caster sugar

¾ tsp easy-blend dried yeast

1 tbsp olive oil

90ml (3fl oz) warm water

FOR THE FILLING

200g (7oz) spinach leaves, wilted and drained

125g (4½ oz) cooked ham, chopped

125g (4½ oz) mozzarella, torn into pieces

handful of torn basil leaves

1 Sift the flour, salt, and sugar into a bowl. Add the yeast. Stir in the oil and enough warm water to form a soft but not sticky dough. Knead gently on a lightly floured surface for several minutes until smooth and elastic. Return to the bowl, cover with oiled cling film, and leave in a warm place for about 40 minutes until the dough has doubled in bulk.

2 Preheat the oven to its highest setting. Very lightly oil a baking tray and put it in the oven to get hot. Turn out the dough on a floured surface and knock it back by re-kneading briefly. Roll out thinly to a round, about 25cm (10in) diameter, and transfer to the hot baking tray, spreading it out firmly again.

3 Squeeze any remaining liquid from the spinach and spread it over half the pizza base, leaving about 1cm (½ in) around the edge. Top with the ham, mozzarella, and basil, then dampen all around the edge of the pizza with water. Fold one half of the pizza over the other, seal the edges together with your fingers, then sprinkle the top with a little water. Bake for 15–20 minutes, or until golden and crispy.

Calzone with peppers, capers, and olives

Black olives and capers give this meal a tapenade-style twist. This is a wonderful way to use up any leftovers from the fridge.

🍴 20 MINS, PLUS RISING

🍲 15–20 MINS

MAKES 4

1 quantity basic pizza dough divided into 4 balls

olive oil, for greasing

plain flour, for dusting

semolina, for sprinkling

10-12 ready-roasted peppers from a jar, drained and chopped

10-12 pitted black olives, roughly chopped

4 tsp capers, rinsed

8-10 tbsp ricotta cheese or mozzarella, torn into pieces

salt and freshly ground black pepper

1 Preheat the oven to 240°C (475°F/Gas 9). Very lightly grease a baking tray and place it in the oven to heat.

2 Place the balls of dough on a floured surface and use a rolling pin to roll them out as thin as you can – about 25–30cm (10–12in) in diameter. Sprinkle the hot baking tray with semolina and transfer the dough onto it. Remember to wear an oven mitt before transferring the dough, as the baking tray will be hot. Set the tray on a heat-resistant surface, like a wooden cutting board. Then, quickly lower the dough onto the centre of the tray, leaving at least an inch and a half of free space around the rim, so it's easier to work with.

3 Spoon the peppers, olives, capers, and ricotta cheese or mozzarella onto one half of the pizza bases, leaving about 1cm (½ in) around the edge. Season well with salt and pepper. Dampen the edges of the pizzas with a little water, then fold one half of the pizzas over the other, and seal together with your fingers. Sprinkle the top with a little water, then bake for 15–20 minutes or until golden and crispy.

Brown soda bread

This Irish bread has a light, cake-like texture. It requires no kneading, so is a wonderfully effort-free loaf to make.

🕙 10-15 MINS

🍲 35-40 MINS

MAKES 1 LOAF

unsalted butter, for greasing

500g (1lb 2oz) stone-ground strong wholemeal flour, plus extra for dusting

1½ tsp bicarbonate of soda

1½ tsp salt

500ml (16fl oz) buttermilk, plus extra if needed

1 Preheat the oven to 200°C (400°F/Gas 6). Grease a baking sheet with butter. Sift the flour, bicarbonate of soda, and salt into a large bowl, tipping in any bran left in the sieve. Mix thoroughly and make a well in the centre.

2 Gradually pour the buttermilk into the centre of the well.

With your hands, quickly draw in the flour to make a soft, slightly sticky dough. Do not overwork the dough. Add a little more buttermilk if it seems dry.

3 Turn the dough out onto a floured surface, and quickly shape into a round loaf. Put the loaf on the baking sheet, and pat it down into a round, about 5cm (2in) high. Make a cross 1cm (½ in) deep in the top of the loaf with a very sharp knife or scalpel.

4 Bake the loaf in the preheated oven for 35–40 minutes, until golden brown. Turn it over and tap the bottom; it should sound hollow when cooked. Transfer to a wire rack and let it cool slightly. It is best served warm from the oven, or the next day as very good toast.

Dinner rolls

You can shape these rolls however you prefer; an assortment of shapes looks attractive in a basket.

🕙 45-55 MINS, PLUS RISING AND PROVING

🍲 15-18 MINS

❄ FREEZABLE

MAKES 16

150ml (5fl oz) whole milk

3 tsp dried yeast

60g (2oz) unsalted butter, cut into cubes, plus extra for greasing

2 tbsp caster sugar

2 whole eggs, plus 1 yolk for glazing

2 tsp salt

550g (1¼ lb) strong white bread flour, plus extra for dusting

poppy seeds, for sprinkling (optional)

1 Bring the milk to the boil. Put 4 tbsp into a small bowl and sprinkle with the yeast. Leave for 5 minutes to dissolve, stirring once. Add the butter and sugar to the remaining milk in the pan until melted. Cool to warm.

2 In a bowl, lightly beat the eggs. Add the sweetened milk, salt, and dissolved yeast. Gradually stir in the flour to get a soft, slightly sticky dough. Knead on a floured surface for 5–7 minutes until elastic.

3 Put in a greased bowl, cover, and leave in a warm place for 1–1½ hours until doubled in size. Grease 2 baking sheets. Put the dough on a floured surface and knock it back. Cut into 16 pieces.

4 For round rolls, roll a piece to form a smooth ball. For a knot, roll into a rope, then shape into an "8". For a "snail", wind into a spiral.

5 Put on the baking sheets. Leave in a warm place for 30 minutes. Preheat the oven to 220°C (425°F/Gas 7). Beat the yolk with 1 tbsp of water, brush the rolls, and sprinkle with poppy seeds (if using). Bake for 15–18 minutes. Serve warm.

Brazilian cheese rolls

Crisp on the outside and chewy within, these "pão de queijo" are a popular street food in their native land.

🥄 **10 MINS**

🍲 **30 MINS**

❄ **FREEZABLE**

SPECIAL EQUIPMENT

food processor

MAKES 16

120ml (4fl oz) whole milk

3-4 tbsp sunflower oil

1 tsp salt

250g (9oz) tapioca (manioc or cassava) flour, plus extra for dusting

2 eggs, beaten, plus extra for glazing

125g (4½ oz) Parmesan cheese, grated

1 Put the milk, oil, 120ml (4fl oz) of water, and the salt in a small saucepan and bring to the boil. Put the flour into a large bowl and quickly mix in the hot liquid. The mixture will be very claggy and stick together. Set aside to cool.

2 Preheat the oven to 190°C (375°F/Gas 5). Once the tapioca mixture has cooled, put it into a food processor with a blade attachment. Add the eggs and process until the lumps disappear and it is a smooth paste. Add the cheese and process until the mixture is sticky and elastic.

3 Turn the mixture out onto a well-floured work surface and knead for 2–3 minutes until smooth and pliable. Divide into 16 equal pieces. Roll each into golf ball-sized balls and place, spaced well apart, on a baking sheet lined with baking parchment.

4 Brush the balls with a little beaten egg, and bake in the middle of the oven for 30 minutes until well risen and golden brown. Remove from the oven and cool for a few minutes before eating. These are best eaten the same day they are made, preferably still warm.

HOW TO FREEZE

These can be open-frozen on the baking sheet at the end of step 3, transferred to freezer bags and frozen for up to 6 months. Simply defrost for 30 minutes and bake as in step 4.

Tortillas

A great alternative to bread, these classic Mexican flatbreads are simple
to make and far tastier than any ready-made tortilla.

🥄 **10 MINS, PLUS RESTING**

🍲 **15-20 MINS**

❄️ **FREEZABLE**

MAKES 8

FOR THE CRUST

300g (10oz) plain flour,
  plus extra for dusting

1 scant tsp salt

½ tsp baking powder

50g (1¾ oz) lard or white vegetable
  fat, chilled and diced, plus extra
  for greasing

1 Place the flour, salt, and baking
  powder into a large bowl. Add
the lard and rub it with your hands
until the mixture resembles fine
crumbs. Add 150ml (5fl oz) of warm
water. Bring the mixture together to
form a rough, soft dough. Turn it out
onto a lightly floured work surface
and knead for 2–3 minutes until
smooth. Place the dough in a
greased bowl, cover with cling film,
and rest in a warm place for 1 hour.

2 Turn the dough out onto a
  floured work surface and
divide it into 8 equal portions.
Take 1 piece and leave the others
covered with cling film to prevent
them from drying. Roll each piece
of dough out thinly to a circle
about 20–25cm (8–10in) in
diameter. Stack the rolled tortillas
in a pile, placing a piece of cling
film or parchment between each.

3 Heat a frying pan over a
  medium heat. Take a tortilla
and dry fry for 1 minute. Turn it
over and continue to fry until both
sides are cooked and browned in
places. Transfer to a wire rack and
repeat to cook all the remaining
tortillas. Serve warm or cool.

Pitta bread

These Middle Eastern flatbreads, best served warm, are essential
for serving with salads and dips, such as hummus.

**20 MINS, PLUS RISING
AND PROVING**

10 MINS

FREEZABLE

MAKES 8

500g (1lb 2oz) strong white bread
flour, plus extra for dusting

1 tsp fast-action dried yeast

1 tsp caster sugar

1 tsp salt

4 tbsp olive oil, plus extra for
greasing

1 Mix together the flour, yeast,
sugar, and salt in a large bowl.
Make a well in the centre and add
the olive oil and 300ml (10fl oz)
lukewarm water. Using a wooden
spoon, start mixing gently to
combine the ingredients, and
then mix and knead together for
5 minutes or until it forms a smooth
dough. Cover with a clean tea towel
and place the dough in a warm
place for 1 hour or until it has
doubled in size.

2 Dust the work surface with
flour and knead the dough
briefly until smooth. Divide into
8 equal pieces and roll each out
into a thin oval shape, about 20cm
(8in) long. Grease 2 large baking
trays and place 4 dough ovals on
each. Cover with oiled cling film
and leave in a warm place for 20
minutes or until the dough is
slightly risen.

3 Preheat the oven to 220°C
(425°F/Gas 7). Brush the tops
of the pittas with a little oil and
bake for 10 minutes or until puffed
and golden brown. Carefully
transfer to a wire rack and
serve while still warm.

Walnut and rosemary loaf

A perfect combination of flavours; the texture of the nuts is fabulous here. It is very good eaten with goat's cheese.

🥄 **20 MINS, PLUS PROVING**

🍲 **30–40 MINS**

❄️ **FREEZABLE**

MAKES 2 LOAVES

3 tsp dried yeast

1 tsp granulated sugar

450g (1lb) strong white bread flour, plus extra for dusting

1 tsp salt

3 tbsp olive oil, plus 2 tsp extra for oiling and glazing

175g (6oz) walnuts, chopped

3 tbsp finely chopped rosemary leaves

1 Mix the yeast and sugar in a small bowl, then stir in 100ml (3½ fl oz) of warm water. Leave for 10–15 minutes, or until the mixture becomes creamy.

2 Put the flour in a bowl with the salt and the oil, then add the yeast mixture and 200ml (7fl oz) of warm water. Mix until it comes together to form a dough. Knead on a floured surface for 15 minutes. Knead in the nuts and

rosemary, then put in an oiled bowl. Cover with a tea towel. Leave in a warm place for 1½ hours until doubled.

3 Knock the air out of the dough and knead for a few more minutes. Halve it, and shape each half into a 15cm (6in) round loaf. Cover with a towel and leave for 30 minutes to rise. Preheat the oven to 230°C (450°F/Gas 8) and oil a large baking sheet.

4 When the dough has doubled, brush with oil and place on the baking sheet. Bake on the

middle shelf of the oven for 30–40 minutes until the loaves sound hollow when tapped on the base. Cool on a wire rack.

COOKING FOR A CROWD

If you are entertaining, try forming the proven dough into individual-sized rolls for easy portion control. Leave them to rise, well spaced out on a baking tray, as in step 2, then bake for 20-25 minutes, until well risen and golden brown.

Quick pumpkin bread

Grated pumpkin keeps this bread moist for up to 3 days. Wrap in greaseproof paper and store in the fridge.

🥣 20 MINS

🍲 50 MINS

❄️ FREEZABLE

MAKES 1 LOAF

300g (10oz) plain flour, plus extra for dusting

100g (3½ oz) wholemeal self-raising flour

1 tsp bicarbonate of soda

½ tsp fine salt

125g (4¼ oz) pumpkin or butternut squash, peeled, deseeded, and roughly grated

30g (1oz) pumpkin seeds

300ml (10fl oz) buttermilk

1 Preheat the oven to 220°C (425°F/Gas 7). In a bowl, mix the flours, bicarbonate of soda, and salt. Add the pumpkin and seeds, and stir. Pour in the buttermilk to form a dough.

2 Knead the dough on a floured surface for 2 minutes until it forms a smooth mass. You may need to add more flour. Shape the dough into a 15cm (6in) round. Place on a lined baking sheet.

3 Use a sharp knife to slash a cross into the top. This helps the bread to rise when baking. Cook for 30 minutes in the centre of the oven until risen. Reduce the oven temperature to 200°C (400°F/Gas 6). Cook for a further 20 minutes. The base should sound hollow when tapped. Cool on a wire rack for at least 20 minutes before serving.

Sweet potato and rosemary rolls

The gentle, aromatic scent of rosemary makes these rolls something special. Eat them warm, with butter.

🥣 20 MINS

🍲 20–25 MINS

❄️ FREEZABLE

MAKES 8

300g (10oz) plain flour, plus extra for dusting

100g (3½ oz) wholemeal self-raising flour

1 tsp bicarbonate of soda

½ tsp fine salt

freshly ground black pepper

140g (5oz) sweet potato, finely grated

1 tsp finely chopped rosemary leaves

250ml (9fl oz) buttermilk

1 Preheat the oven to 220°C (425°F/Gas 7). Line a baking sheet with baking parchment. In a bowl, mix the flours, bicarbonate of soda, salt, and pepper. Mix in the sweet potato and rosemary.

2 Stir in the buttermilk, bringing the mixture together to form a loose dough. Turn it out onto a floured surface and knead for 2 minutes to form a smooth dough. You may need a little more flour.

3 Divide into 8 equal pieces, and shape each into a tight round. Flatten the tops and cut a cross in the centres with a sharp knife to help them rise in the oven.

4 Place the rolls on the lined baking tray. Cook in the middle of the oven for 20–25 minutes until the rolls are well risen and golden brown. Transfer to a wire rack and allow to cool for at least 10 minutes before serving.

Courgette and feta loaf

This simple, savoury loaf is the perfect, piquant accompaniment to a bowl of home-made soup on a cold day.

 20 MINS

40–45 MINS

❄ **FREEZABLE**

MAKES 1 LOAF

100ml (3½ fl oz) sunflower oil

250g (9oz) courgette, finely grated

½ tsp salt

125g (4½ oz) plain flour

75g (2½ oz) wholemeal flour

1½ tsp baking powder

3 eggs, lightly beaten

3-4 tbsp whole milk

2 heaped tbsp chopped parsley leaves

100g (3½ oz) feta cheese, chopped

1 Preheat the oven to 180°C (350°F/Gas 4). Oil a 450g (1lb) loaf tin and line the base with baking parchment. Put the grated courgettes into a sieve and toss them in the salt.

2 Sift the flours and baking powder into a large bowl and season well. Whisk the eggs, oil, and milk, and mix into the flour.

3 Rinse the courgettes under cold water and press them down well in the sieve to remove as much water as possible. Fold the courgettes, parsley, and feta into the loaf mixture.

4 Pour the mixture into the prepared loaf tin and bake in the centre of the hot oven for 40–45 minutes, until a skewer inserted into the centre comes out clean.

5 Remove the loaf from the oven and turn it out onto a wire rack. Allow it to cool for at least 10 minutes before cutting into it to serve warm; alternatively, allow it to cool completely before serving. If keeping the loaf for more than 1 day, wrap in cling film and store in the fridge for up to 3 days, or freeze for up to 12 weeks.

CLEVER WITH LEFTOVERS

Although best served warm the same day, this bread is also great toasted, spread with cream cheese, and topped with sliced cucumber and freshly ground black pepper for a quick, healthy lunch.

Parsnip and parmesan bread

A perfect combination of flavours to serve with a bowl of warming soup on a cold winter's day.

- 🥣 20 MINS
- 🍲 50 MINS
- ❄️ FREEZABLE

MAKES 1 LOAF

300g (10oz) plain flour

100g (3½ oz) wholemeal self-raising flour

1 tsp bicarbonate of soda

50g (1¾ oz) Parmesan cheese, finely grated

salt and freshly ground black pepper

150g (5½ oz) parsnip, coarsely grated

300ml (10fl oz) buttermilk

1 Preheat the oven to 220°C (425°F/Gas 7). Line a baking tray with baking parchment. In a bowl, mix together the flours, bicarbonate of soda, and Parmesan cheese together with some salt and pepper. Roughly chop the grated parsnip to reduce the size of the shreds. Add it to the bowl, mixing it in well.

2 Make a well in the centre of the dry ingredients and gently stir in the buttermilk, bringing the mixture together to form a loose dough. Use your hands to bring the mixture together into a ball, then turn it out onto a floured work surface and knead for 2 minutes until it forms a smooth dough. You may need to add a little extra flour at this stage.

3 Shape the dough into a round, about 15cm (6in) in diameter. Slash a cross in the top of the dough with a sharp knife to allow the bread to rise easily when baking.

4 Place the dough on the baking tray and cook in the middle of the oven for 30 minutes to create a good crust. Reduce the temperature to 200°C (400°F/Gas 6) and bake for 20 minutes until well risen, golden brown, and a skewer inserted into the middle emerges clean. Transfer to a wire rack and allow it to cool for at least 20 minutes before serving.

Sweet potato paratha

These flatbreads are so quick to make, it's worth doubling up and freezing half layered between greaseproof paper.

- 🥣 20 MINS PLUS RESTING
- 🍲 15–20 MINS
- ❄️ FREEZABLE

MAKES 4

300g (10oz) chapatti flour

salt

50g (1¾ oz) unsalted butter, melted and cooled

For the stuffing

250g (9oz) sweet potato, peeled and diced

1 tbsp sunflower oil, plus extra for brushing

½ red onion, finely chopped

2 garlic cloves, crushed

1 tbsp finely chopped red chilli, or to taste

1 tbsp finely chopped fresh root ginger

2 heaped tbsp chopped coriander

½ tsp garam masala

1 To make the dough for the paratha, sift the flour and ½ tsp salt into a bowl. Add the butter and 150ml (5fl oz) water, and bring the mixture together to form a soft dough. Knead for 5 minutes, then let the dough rest, covered, for 1 hour.

2 To make the stuffing, boil or steam the sweet potato for about 7 minutes until tender. Drain it well. Heat the oil in a frying pan over a medium heat, add the red onion, and cook for 3–4 minutes until soft. Add the garlic, chilli, and ginger, and continue to cook for 1–2 minutes.

3 Add the cooked onion mixture to the sweet potato and mash well. Add the coriander, garam masala, and a good seasoning of salt, and beat until smooth. Set aside to cool.

4 When the dough has rested, divide it into 4 pieces. Knead each piece and roll it out into a circle, around 10cm (4in) in diameter. Put a quarter of the stuffing in the middle. Pull the edges up around it, forming a purse shape.

5 Pinch the edges together to seal in the stuffing, turn the dough over, and roll it out into a circle, about 18cm (7in) in diameter, taking care not to roll too hard. If the filling bursts out, wipe it off and pinch the dough together to reseal the paratha.

6 Heat a large cast-iron frying pan or griddle over a medium heat. Fry the parathas for 2 minutes on each side, turning occasionally to make sure they are well cooked and browning in places. Once they have cooked on each side once, brush the surface with a little oil before turning them again. Serve immediately alongside a curry, or as a light lunch dish with a green salad.

Black olive and pepper ciabatta

A good ciabatta should be well risen and crusty, with large air pockets.
Using black olives and roasted red peppers in this easy-to-master
recipe makes for an unusual, tasty loaf studded with black and red.

🥣 **40 MINS PLUS RISING
AND PROVING**

🍲 **30 MINS**

❄️ **FREEZABLE**

MAKES 2

2 tsp dried yeast

2 tbsp olive oil

450g (1lb) strong white bread flour

1 tsp sea salt

50g (1¾ oz) stoned black olives,
drained, roughly chopped, and
dried with kitchen paper

1 red pepper, roasted, peeled and
roughly chopped

1 Dissolve the yeast with 350ml
(12fl oz) warm water in a bowl,
then add the oil. Put the flour and
salt in a separate mixing bowl.
Make a well in the centre of the
flour, pour in the yeast mixture, and
stir together to form a soft dough.

2 Knead the dough for 10
minutes on a floured work
surface, then stretch it out thinly
and scatter over the olives and
pepper. Bring the sides of the
dough together to cover the olives
and pepper. Knead the dough
briefly until the olives and pepper
are fully incorporated. Put the
dough in an oiled bowl, cover
loosely with cling film, and leave
to rise in a warm place for up to 2
hours until doubled in size.

3 Turn the dough out onto a
floured work surface and
knock it back. Divide it into 2
pieces, then knead and mould each
piece into a 30 x 10cm (12 x 4in)
traditional slipper shape. Place
the loaves on a lined baking sheet,
cover with cling film and a tea
towel, and leave for 1 hour until
they have doubled in size.

4 Preheat the oven to 230°C
(450°F/Gas 8). Spray the loaves
with a mist of water and bake in
the centre of the oven for 30
minutes until golden brown; spray
the loaves with water every 10
minutes. The bread is cooked
when the base sounds hollow
when tapped. Cool for 30 minutes
before cutting.

Stuffed ciabatta

One of the simplest breads to master, a good ciabatta should be
well risen and crusty, with large air pockets.

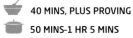 **40 MINS, PLUS PROVING**

50 MINS–1 HR 5 MINS

FREEZABLE

MAKES 2 LOAVES

2 tsp dried yeast

6 tbsp olive oil, plus extra for
greasing

450g (1lb) strong white bread flour,
plus extra for dusting

1 tsp sea salt

1 red pepper, chopped into 1cm
(½ in) cubes

1 yellow pepper, chopped into 1cm
(½ in) cubes

1 red onion, chopped into 1cm
(½ in) cubes

1 aubergine, chopped into 1cm
(½ in) cubes

freshly ground black pepper

2 heaped tbsp pesto

1 Dissolve the yeast in 350ml
(12fl oz) of warm water, then
add 4 tbsp of the oil. Put the flour
and salt in a bowl. Stir in the yeast
mixture to form a dough. Knead
for 10 minutes, put in an oiled bowl,
cover, and leave in a warm place
for 2 hours, or until doubled in size.

2 Preheat the oven to 230°C
(450°F/Gas 8). Mix the
vegetables and remaining oil and
season. Bake for 30–40 minutes,
until crisp, then leave to cool.

3 Turn the dough out onto a
floured surface and knock it
back. Form it into two 30 x 20cm
(12 x 8in) rectangles. Top each with
half the pesto and vegetables, then
roll the loaves up like Swiss rolls.

4 Place, seam-side down, on
floured baking sheets and tuck
the ends under. Cover loosely with
cling film and a towel. Leave for 1
hour, or until doubled in size.

5 Preheat the oven to 230°C
(450°F/Gas 8). Spray the loaves
with water. Bake for 20–25 minutes
until hollow-sounding when
tapped. Cool on wire racks.

Naan bread

Although this familiar Indian flatbread is traditionally cooked in a tandoor oven, a conventional oven also provides authentic results.

🥣 **20 MINS, PLUS RISING**

🍲 **7-8 MINS**

❄ **FREEZABLE**

MAKES 6

50g (1¾ oz) ghee or butter

500g (1lb 2oz) strong white bread flour, plus extra for dusting

2 tsp dried yeast

1 tsp caster sugar

1 tsp salt

2 tsp black onion (nigella) seeds

100ml (3½ fl oz) full-fat plain yogurted, plus extra for greasing

1 Heat the ghee or butter in a small saucepan until melted. Set aside. In a large bowl, mix together the flour, yeast, sugar, salt, and onion seeds. Make a well. Add 200ml (7fl oz) of lukewarm water, the yogurt, and the melted ghee. Draw in the flour and mix gently with a wooden spoon to combine. Keep mixing for 5 minutes until it forms a rough dough. Cover and keep warm until doubled; about 1 hour. Preheat the oven to 240°C (475°F/Gas 9).

2 Place 2 baking trays in the oven. Knock back the dough.

Knead the dough on a floured surface until smooth. Divide into 4 equal pieces. Roll each piece into an oval shape about 25cm (10in) long. Transfer the bread to the trays and bake for 6–7 minutes until well puffed. Remember to wear an oven mitt before transferring the bread, as the baking tray will be hot. Set the tray on a heat-resistant surface, like a wooden cutting board. Then, quickly lower the bread onto the centre of the tray, leaving at least an inch and a half of free space around the rim, so it's easier to work with.

3 Preheat the grill to its hottest setting. Transfer the bread to the grill pan. Cook the naans for 30–40 seconds on each side or until they brown and blister. When grilling, take care not to put the breads too close to the heat, to prevent burning. Transfer to a wire rack and serve warm.

Chapatis

In India, these flat, unleavened breads are cooked in a concave pan called a tava but, a cast-iron frying pan works just as well.

 **30 MINS PLUS RESTING**

10 MINS

SPECIAL EQUIPMENT

tava or heavy, cast-iron frying pan

MAKES 8

250g (9oz) chapati flour or wholemeal plain flour, plus extra for dusting

1 tsp salt

ghee or melted butter, for brushing

1 Sift the flour into a bowl and discard any bran left in the sieve. Make a well in the centre, add 40ml (3 tbsp) cold water, and mix together. Work in the salt, then add another 60ml (2fl oz) cold water and mix until the dough starts to come together.

2 Gradually add another 60ml (2fl oz) cold water to make a sticky dough. Keep kneading the dough in the bowl until it is firm, elastic, and less sticky.

3 Cover with a clean tea towel and leave to rest for 15 minutes or until the dough becomes firmer, and no longer sticky.

4 Dust your hands with flour and pull off egg-sized pieces of dough. Shape into balls, then roll out into rounds 18cm (7in) in diameter.

5 Heat the ungreased frying pan and cook the chapatis for 30 seconds on each side or until golden and speckled. Remove from the pan, brush with ghee or melted butter, keeping them warm as you cook the rest.

Wholewheat pooris

These deep-fried, puffed Indian breads are ideal served with curries.
Chapati flour is easily available from Asian shops.

🥣 **15 MINS, PLUS RESTING**

🍲 **16 MINS**

❄️ **FREEZABLE**

MAKES 8

250g (9oz) wholewheat chapati
   flour or plain wholemeal flour

1 tsp salt

½ tsp caster sugar

1 tsp black onion seeds

½ tsp cumin seeds

2 tsp ghee

vegetable oil, for deep-frying

1 Place the flour, salt, sugar, onion seeds, and cumin seeds in a large mixing bowl and mix together, then rub in the ghee with your fingertips.

2 Gradually add 120ml (4fl oz) cold water and mix to make a stiff dough. Knead until smooth, then wrap in cling film and leave to rest for at least 30 minutes.

3 Divide the dough into 8 equal pieces and roll each into balls. Heat the oil to 180°C (350°F).

4 Roll each piece of dough into a 12.5cm (5in) round and deep-fry each for 2 minutes or until puffed up, crisp, and golden on both sides. Drain on kitchen paper and serve hot.

Grissini

Tradition has it that breadsticks should be pulled to the length of the baker's arm... these are more manageable!

40-45 MINS PLUS RISING

15-18 MINS

MAKES 32

2½ tsp dried yeast

425g (15oz) strong white bread
    flour, plus extra for dusting

1 tbsp caster sugar

2 tsp salt

2 tbsp extra virgin olive oil

45g (1½ oz) sesame seeds

1 Sprinkle the yeast over 4 tbsp of warm water. Leave for 5 minutes, stirring once. Put the flour, sugar, and salt in a bowl. Add the yeast, 250ml (9fl oz) of warm water, and the oil. Mix to make a sticky dough.

2 Knead on a floured surface for 5–7 minutes until very smooth and elastic. Let rest for 5 minutes.

3 Roll the dough out to 40 x 15cm (16 x 6in). Cover it with a damp tea towel. Leave in a warm place for 1½ hours, until doubled in size.

4 Preheat the oven to 220°C (425°F/Gas 7). Dust 3 baking sheets with flour. Brush the dough with water and sprinkle with the sesame seeds.

5 With a sharp knife, cut the dough into 32 strips, each 1cm (½ in) wide. Stretch 1 strip to the width of a baking sheet. Set it on the baking sheet. Arrange the remaining strips 2cm (¾ in) apart. Bake for 15–18 minutes until golden and crisp. These keep in an airtight container for up to 2 days.

PREPARE AHEAD

In step 3 the rectangle of dough can be left to rise slowly overnight in the fridge, if it is more convenient. Shape and bake the grissini the next day.

Pretzels

These German breads are great fun to make, and the two-stage glazing method gives an authentic chewy result.

🥄 **50 MINS, PLUS PROVING**

🍲 **20 MINS**

❄️ **FREEZABLE**

MAKES 16

350g (12oz) strong white bread
flour, plus extra for dusting

150g (5½ oz) plain flour

1 tsp salt

2 tbsp caster sugar

2 tsp dried yeast

1 tbsp sunflower oil, plus extra
for greasing

FOR THE GLAZE

¼ tsp bicarbonate of soda

2 tbsp coarse sea salt
or sesame seeds

1 egg, lightly beaten, for glazing

1 Put the 2 types of flour, salt, and sugar into a bowl. Sprinkle the yeast over 300ml (10fl oz) of warm water. Stir, leave for 5 minutes, then add the oil. Gradually pour into the flour, stirring to form a soft dough.

2 Knead for 10 minutes until soft and pliable. Put in an oiled bowl. Cover loosely with cling film and leave in a warm place for 1–2 hours until nearly doubled in size.

Turn out onto a floured work surface, and gently knock it back.

3 With a sharp knife, cut the dough into 16 equal pieces. Take each piece and roll it to make a log shape. Continue to roll the dough towards each end, until it is 45cm (18in) long.

4 Take each end of the dough and cross it over the other, forming a heart shape. Now twist the ends around each other as though they had linked arms.

5 Secure the ends to the sides of the pretzel. Repeat to make 16, placing them on baking sheets lined with parchment. Cover with

cling film and a tea towel. Leave in a warm place for 30 minutes to puff.

6 Preheat the oven to 200°C (400°F/Gas 6). Mix the soda in 2 tbsp boiling water. Brush the pretzels with the mixture. This gives them a dark colour and chewy exterior. Scatter flakes of sea salt or sesame seeds over the brushed pretzels. Bake for 15 minutes.

7 Remove from the oven and brush with beaten egg. Bake for 5 minutes. Remove from the oven; they should be shiny. Let cool on a wire rack for at least 5 minutes before serving.

Pane di patate

Bread made with mashed potato has a soft crust and moist centre. Here, the dough is coated in butter and baked.

50-55 MINS, PLUS RISING AND PROVING

40-45 MINS

FREEZABLE

SPECIAL EQUIPMENT

1.75-litre (3-pint) ring mould, or 25cm (10in) round cake tin and 250ml (9fl oz) ramekin

MAKES 1 LOAF

250g (9oz) potatoes, peeled, and each cut into 2-3 pieces

2½ tsp dried yeast

125g (4½ oz) unsalted butter, plus extra for greasing

1 large bunch of chives, snipped

2 tbsp caster sugar

2 tsp salt

425g (15oz) strong white bread flour, plus extra for dusting

1 Simmer the potatoes in water until tender. Drain, reserving 250ml (9fl oz) of the liquid. Mash with a potato masher. Let them cool.

2 In a small bowl, sprinkle the yeast over 4 tbsp of warm water. Stir it once and leave for 5 minutes until dissolved. Melt half the butter in a pan. Put the reserved potato liquid, mashed potato, dissolved yeast, and melted butter into a bowl. Mix in the chives, sugar, and salt.

3 Stir in half the flour and mix well. Add the remaining flour, 60g (2oz) at a time, mixing well after each addition, until the dough pulls away from the sides of the bowl. It should be soft and slightly sticky. Knead the dough on a floured work surface for 5–7 minutes, until smooth and elastic.

4 Put the dough in a greased bowl, cover with a damp tea towel, and leave in a warm place for 1–½ hours, until doubled.

5 Grease a 1.75-litre (3-pint) ring mould or 25cm (10in) round cake tin. If using a tin, grease the outside of a 250ml (9fl oz) ramekin and place it upside down in the centre. Melt the remaining butter. Turn the dough out and knock back. Cover and let rest for 5 minutes. Pinch off about 30 walnut-sized pieces. Roll each piece into a smooth ball.

6 Put a few balls into the dish of melted butter and turn to coat. Transfer to the mould or tin. Repeat with the remaining dough. Cover with a dry tea towel, and leave in a warm place for about 40 minutes, until the dough has risen to fill the mould or tin.

7 Preheat the oven to 190°C (375°F/Gas 5). Bake the bread for 40–45 minutes until it is golden brown. Let it cool slightly, then carefully unmould. Serve, pulling the bread apart, while still warm.

Zwiebelkuchen

The combination of soured cream and caraway seeds contrast well
with the sweet, melting onions in this recipe.

 30 MINS, PLUS PROVING

1 HR–1 HR 5 MINS

FREEZABLE

SPECIAL EQUIPMENT

26 x 32cm (10 x 13in) baking tray
with raised edges

SERVES 8

FOR THE CRUST

4 tsp dried yeast

3 tbsp olive oil, plus extra for
greasing

400g (14oz) strong white bread
flour, plus extra for dusting

1 tsp salt

FOR THE FILLING

50g (1¾ oz) unsalted butter

2 tbsp olive oil

600g (1lb 5oz) onions, finely sliced

½ tsp caraway seeds

salt and freshly ground
black pepper

150ml (5fl oz) soured cream

150ml (5fl oz) crème fraîche

3 eggs, lightly beaten

1 tbsp plain flour

75g (2½ oz) smoked streaky bacon
rashers, chopped

1 To make the crust, dissolve
the yeast in 225ml (7½ fl oz) of
warm water. Add the oil. Sift the
flour and salt into a large bowl.
Make a well and pour in the wet
ingredients. Use your hands to
form a soft dough. Turn out onto a
floured work surface and knead for
10 minutes until elastic.

2 Place the dough in an oiled
bowl, cover with cling film,
and leave in a warm place for 1–2
hours until doubled in size.

3 For the filling, heat the butter
and oil in a large, heavy-based
saucepan. Put in the onions and
caraway seeds, and season. Cover
and cook gently for 20 minutes, until
soft. Remove the lid and cook for 5
minutes until liquid evaporates.

4 In a separate bowl, whisk
together the soured cream,
crème fraîche, eggs, and plain flour,
and season well. Mix in the cooked
onions and set aside to cool.

5 When the dough has risen,
turn it out onto a floured work
surface and knock it back. Lightly
oil a 26 x 32cm (10 x 13in) baking
tray with raised edges. Roll the
dough out to roughly the size of
the tray and line the tray with it.
Cover with lightly oiled cling film
and leave in a warm place for 30
minutes until puffy.

6 Preheat the oven to 200°C
(400°F/Gas 6). Gently push
down the dough. Spread the filling
over and sprinkle the bacon on top.

7 Place on the top shelf of the
oven, and bake for 35–40
minutes until golden. Remove
and leave to cool for 5 minutes
before serving warm or cold.

Anadama cornbread

This dark, sweet cornbread originally hails from New England.
It is curiously sweet and savoury at the same time.

25 MINS, PLUS PROVING

45–50 MINS

FREEZABLE

SERVES 4

120ml (4fl oz) whole milk

75g (2½ oz) polenta or fine
yellow cornmeal

50g (1¾ oz) unsalted butter,
softened

100g (3½ oz) black treacle

2 tsp dried yeast

450g (1lb) plain flour, plus extra
for dusting

1 tsp salt

vegetable oil, for greasing

1 egg, lightly beaten, for glazing

1 Heat the milk and 120ml (4fl oz) of water in a small saucepan. Bring to the boil and add the polenta. Cook for 1–2 minutes or until it thickens, then remove from the heat. Stir in the butter until well mixed. Beat in the treacle, then set aside to cool.

2 Dissolve the yeast in 100ml (3½ fl oz) of warm water and stir well. Sift the flour and salt into a bowl and make a well. Gradually stir in the polenta mixture, then add the yeast mixture to make a soft, sticky dough.

3 Turn the dough out onto a lightly floured work surface. Knead for about 10 minutes until soft and elastic. It will remain fairly sticky, but should not stick to your hands. Knead in a little flour if it seems too wet. Put the dough in a lightly oiled bowl, cover loosely with cling film, and leave to rise in a warm place for up to 2 hours. The dough will not double in size, but should be very soft and pliable when well risen.

4 Turn the dough out onto a lightly floured work surface and gently knock it back. Knead it briefly and shape it into a flattened oval, tucking the sides underneath the centre of the dough to get a tight, even shape. Place on a large baking tray, and cover loosely with cling film and a clean tea towel. Leave it to rise in a warm place for about 2 hours. The dough is ready to bake when it is tight and well risen, and a finger gently poked into the dough leaves a dent that springs back quickly.

5 Preheat the oven to 180°C (350°F/Gas 4). Place one oven shelf in the middle of the oven, and another below it, close to the bottom. Boil a kettle of water. Brush the loaf with a little beaten egg, and slash the top 2 or 3 times with a sharp knife on the diagonal. Dust the top with flour, if desired, and place it on the middle shelf. Place a roasting pan on the bottom shelf, then quickly pour the boiling water into it and shut the door.

6 Bake for 45–50 minutes until the crust is nicely darkened and the bottom sounds hollow when tapped. Remove from the oven and leave to cool on a wire rack. Serve with Emmental or Gruyère cheese, or buttered and topped with ham and mustard.

Cinnamon rolls

Leave these rolls to prove overnight in the fridge so they are ready to bake in time for a brunch treat.

🥣 40 MINS PLUS PROVING

🍲 25-30 MINS

❄ FREEZABLE

SPECIAL EQUIPMENT

30cm (12in) springform cake tin

MAKES 10-12

120ml (4fl oz) whole milk

100g (3½ oz) unsalted butter, plus extra for greasing

2 tsp dried yeast

50g (1¾ oz) caster sugar

550g (1¼ lb) plain flour, sifted, plus extra for dusting

1 tsp salt

1 egg, plus 2 egg yolks

vegetable oil, for greasing

FOR THE FILLING AND GLAZE

3 tbsp ground cinnamon

100g (3½ oz) soft light brown sugar

25g (scant 1oz) unsalted butter, melted

1 egg, lightly beaten

4 tbsp caster sugarg

1 In a pan, heat 120ml (4fl oz) of water, the milk, and butter until melted. Let it cool to just warm, then whisk in the yeast and 1 tbsp of the sugar. Cover for 10 minutes.

2 Place the flour, salt, and remaining sugar in a large bowl. Make a well in the centre of the dry ingredients and pour in the warm milk mixture. Whisk the egg and egg yolks, and add to the mixture. Combine to form a rough dough. Place on a floured surface and knead for 10 minutes. Add extra flour if it's too sticky.

3 Put in an oiled bowl, cover with cling film, and keep in a warm place for 2 hours until well risen. Meanwhile, prepare the filling by mixing 2 tbsp of the cinnamon with the brown sugar.

4 When the dough has risen, turn it out onto a floured work surface and gently knock it back. Roll it out into a rectangle, measuring about 40 x 30cm (16 x 12in). Brush with the melted butter. Scatter with the filling, leaving a 1cm (½ in) border on one long side. Brush this with the egg.

5 Press the filling with the palm of your hand to ensure it sticks to the dough. Roll the dough up, working towards the egg-brushed border. Do not roll too tightly.

6 Cut into 10–12 equal pieces with a serrated knife, taking care not to squash the rolls. Grease and line a 30cm (12in) springform cake tin. Pack in the rolls, cut-sides up. Cover and prove for 1–2 hours until well risen.

7 Preheat the oven to 180°C (350°F/Gas 4). Brush with egg and bake for 25–30 minutes. Heat 3 tbsp of water with 2 tbsp of the sugar for the glaze until the sugar has dissolved. Brush on the rolls. Sprinkle over the mixed remaining sugar and cinnamon, and turn out onto a wire rack to cool.

Rosemary focaccia

This is a good-tempered dough that can be left in the fridge to rise overnight. Return to room temperature to bake.

🥣 30-35 MINS PLUS RISING AND PROVING

🍲 15-20 MINS

❄️ FREEZABLE

SPECIAL EQUIPMENT

38 x 23cm (15 x 9in) Swiss roll tin

SERVES 6-8

1 tbsp dried yeast

425g (15oz) strong white bread flour, plus extra for dusting

2 tsp salt

leaves from 5-7 rosemary sprigs, two-thirds finely chopped

6 tbsp olive oil, plus extra for greasing

¼ tsp freshly ground black pepper

sea salt flakes

1 Sprinkle the yeast over 4 tbsp of warm water. Leave it for 5 minutes, stirring once. In a large bowl, mix the flour with the salt and make a well in the centre. Add the chopped rosemary, 4 tbsp of the oil, the yeast mixture, pepper, and 240ml (8fl oz) of warm water.

2 Gradually draw in the flour and work it into the other ingredients to form a smooth dough. It should be soft and sticky, so do not be tempted to add more flour to dry it out. Sprinkle the dough lightly with flour and knead it for 5-7 minutes on a floured work surface.

3 When ready, the dough will be very smooth and elastic. Place in an oiled bowl. Cover with a damp tea towel. Leave to rise in a warm place for 1-1½ hours until doubled in size. Put the dough on a floured work surface and knock out the air. Cover with a dry tea towel and let it rest for about 5 minutes.

4 Brush a 38 x 23cm (15 x 9in) Swiss roll tin with oil. Transfer the dough to the tin. With your hands, flatten the dough to fill the tin evenly. Cover with a tea towel and leave to rise in a warm place for 35-45 minutes until it is puffed up.

5 Preheat the oven to 200°C (400°F/Gas 6). Scatter the reserved rosemary leaves on top. With your fingers, poke the dough all over to make deep dimples. Pour the remaining 2 tbsp of oil all over the dough and sprinkle with sea salt flakes. Bake on the top shelf of the oven for 15-20 minutes until browned. Transfer to a wire rack to cool.

Blackberry focaccia

The addition of blackberries turns this classic bread into a lovely sweet dessert, tea-time treat, or as part of a meal on the go.

🥣 **30-35 MINS PLUS RISING AND PROVING**

🍲 **15-20 MINS**

SPECIAL EQUIPMENT

38 x 23cm (15 x 9in) Swiss roll tin

SERVES 6-8

1 tbsp dried yeast

425g (15oz) strong white bread flour, plus extra for dusting

1 tsp salt

3 tbsp caster sugar

90ml (3fl oz) extra virgin olive oil

300g (10oz) blackberries

1 Sprinkle the yeast over 4 tbsp lukewarm water in a small bowl. Leave to stand for 5 minutes until dissolved, stirring once.

2 Put the flour, salt, and 2 tbsp of the sugar in a mixing bowl and mix together. Make a well in the centre of the mix and add the dissolved yeast, 4 tbsp of the oil, and 240ml (8fl oz) lukewarm water. Draw in the flour and mix to form a smooth dough. The dough should be soft and sticky; avoid adding more flour to dry it out.

3 Flour your hands and the dough, and turn it out onto a floured surface. Knead for 5–7 minutes until smooth and elastic. Transfer to an oiled bowl and cover with a damp tea towel. Leave to rise in a warm place for about 1–1½ hours until doubled in bulk.

4 Generously brush the tin with oil. Turn out the dough and knock out the air. Cover with a dry tea towel and leave to rest for 5 minutes. Transfer to the tin,

flattening it with your hands so it fills the tin. Scatter the blackberries over the surface of the dough, cover with the tea towel, and leave to prove in a warm place for 35–45 minutes until puffed.

5 Preheat the oven to 200°C (400°F/Gas 6). Brush the dough with the remaining oil and sprinkle over the rest of the sugar. Bake at the top of the oven for 15–20 minutes, until lightly browned. Cool slightly on a wire rack, then serve warm.

Stollen

This rich, fruity German bread is served at Christmas.
Traditionally it contains marzipan, but this version is simpler.

🥄 **30 MINS, PLUS RISING**

🍲 **50 MINS**

❄️ **FREEZABLE**

SERVES 12

200g (7oz) raisins

100g (3½ oz) currants

100ml (3½ fl oz) rum

400g (14oz) strong white bread
flour, plus extra for dusting

2 tsp dried yeast

60g (2oz) caster sugar

100ml (3½ fl oz) whole milk

½ tsp vanilla extract

pinch of salt

½ tsp mixed spice

2 large eggs, lightly beaten

175g (6oz) unsalted butter, softened
and cut into cubes

200g (7oz) mixed peel

100g (3½oz) ground almonds

icing sugar, for dusting

1 Put the raisins and currants into a large bowl, pour over the rum, and leave to soak overnight. The following day, sift the flour into a large bowl. Make a well in the centre, sprinkle in the yeast, and add a teaspoon of the sugar. Gently heat the milk until lukewarm and pour on top of the yeast. Leave to stand at room temperature for 15 minutes or until it turns frothy.

2 Add the rest of the sugar, the vanilla, salt, mixed spice, eggs, and butter. Mix everything together with a wooden spoon. Knead for 5 minutes until smooth.

3 Transfer to a lightly floured surface. Add the mixed peel, raisins, currants, and almonds, kneading for a few minutes until mixed. Return to the bowl, cover loosely with cling film, and leave to rise in a warm place for 1–1½ hours until doubled in size.

4 Preheat the oven to 160°C (325°F/Gas 3). Line a baking tray with baking parchment. On a floured surface, roll out the dough to make a 30 x 25cm (12 x 10in) rectangle. Fold one long side over, just beyond the middle, then fold over the other long side to overlap

the first, curving it slightly on top to create the stollen shape.

5 Transfer to the baking tray and set aside in a warm place, without draughts, for 1–1½ hours to prove once more, until doubled in size again.

6 Bake in the oven for 50 minutes or until the stollen has risen and is pale golden. Check after 30–35 minutes and, if it seems to be browning too much, cover the loaf loosely with foil. Carefully transfer to a wire rack to cool completely, then dust generously with icing sugar to serve.

Acknowledgments

DK would like to thank:

Editors: Lucy Bannell, Emma Callery, Dorothy Kikon, Scarlett O'Hara, Shashwati Tia Sarkar, Arani Sinha, Suasnnah Steel, Chitra Subramanyam

Art Editors: Alison Gardner, Anchal Kausal, Katherine Raj, Sara Robin, Ivy Roy

New photography: Ian O'Leary, Lis Parsons, William Reavell, Stuart West

Photography art direction: Susan Downing, Geoff Fennell, Lisa Pettibone, Penny Stock

Food styling: Emma-Jane Frost, Paul Jackman, Jane Lawrie, Rosie Reynolds, Penny Stephens

Prop styling: Susan Downing, Liz Hippisley, Wei Tang

Recipe testers: Jane Bamforth, Ramona Andrews, Anna Burges-Lumsden, Amy Carter, Sue Davie, Francesca Dennis, Hulya Erdal, Georgina Fuggle, Jan Fullwood, Claire Greenstreet, Anne Harnan, Richard Harris, Sue Harris, Jo Kerr, Sarah King, Emma Lahaye, Bren Parkins-Knight, Ann Reynolds, Cathy Seward, Rachel Wood, and Amanda Wright.